Why My Wife Thinks I'm an Idiot

Why My Wife Thinks I'm an

IDIOT

The Life and Times of a Sportscaster Dad

MIKE GREENBERG

VILLARD **V** NEW YORK

2007 Villard Books Trade Paperback Edition

Published in the United States by Villard Books, an imprint
of The Random House Publishing Group, a division
of Random House, Inc., New York.

VILLARD and "V" CIRCLED Design are registered trademarks
of Random House, Inc.

Originally published in hardcover in the United States by
Villard Books, an imprint of The Random House Publishing
Group, a division of Random House, Inc., in 2006.

ISBN 978-0-8129-7480-5

Library of Congress Cataloging-in-Publication Data
Greenberg, Mike
Why my wife thinks I'm an idiot: sports, family, and the
pursuit of sanity / Mike Greenberg.
p.   cm.
ISBN 978-0-8129-7480-5
1. Greenberg, Mike.   2. Sportscaster—United States—
Biography.   I. Title.
GV742.42.G72 A35 2006
2005043749

Printed in the United States of America

www.villard.com

1 2 3 4 5 6 7 8 9

Book design by Simon M. Sullivan

This book is for
Nikki and Stephen,
who are my inspiration,

and for **Stacy,**
who lived it with me.
And, through it all, I still see her
face every time I close my eyes.

You have to keep passing the open windows.

—John Irving

Bit by bit, little by little, block by block, we're building it up.

—The Wiggles

Preface to the Paperback Edition

ALL OF MY ADULT LIFE, people have been asking me what it's like to be a professional sportscaster. Until last year, that is, when that question was replaced by a new one.

"What's it like to write a book?"

Well, after much reflection, I think my best answer to that question is this.

Humbling.

And I don't mean that in the superficial way that celebrities often say it, as though flying private jets and being stalked by paparazzi have somehow given them an inferiority complex. No, I mean *genuinely* humbling.

It began the day this book was released in hardcover: March 7, 2006. That day was the fulfillment of a lifelong dream. I have always wanted to be a writer. In fact, this is actually the third book I wrote; it's just the first one I can prove because no one ever published either of the other two. (For the record, they're both brilliant.)

What I really wanted was to walk into a bookstore and buy a copy of my own book. And on that March day, I did just that. As soon as we finished *Mike and Mike in the Morning*, I went straight to the bookstore near my house, one where I had a signing scheduled for three weeks later. My hands were shaking as I turned off the engine of my car. Then a bolt of electricity ran through me when I saw the *huge* picture of me in the window.

COME MEET GREENY, MARCH 28TH!

This was almost too much to believe. I had really done it.

In I went, and quickly I found the enormous display with dozens of copies of my book—*my book*—and I thought to myself: *This might be the greatest moment of my life.*

The display was so neatly stacked it felt like a shame to disturb it, but eventually I did remove one book from the mound, with great care, and off I went to the register.

(Now, before we go on, please take another look at the front cover of this book. You'll notice that I'm hard to miss on it. The hardcover had the same photo on the jacket—quite possibly the most self indulgent package in the history of publishing. That made what follows all the more difficult to explain. But I swear to you that it happened exactly this way.)

I handed the book and a credit card—bearing my name, I might add—to the lovely young lady behind the register. She took a long look at the cover . . .

And then she took a long look at me . . .

And she smiled. . . .

And then she said: "He's going to be here at the end of the month, if you'd like to meet him."

It was a painful illustration of something I came to learn in the weeks and months that followed: Having a book published does not exempt one from being treated like a schnook.

The good news, though, is that my experience in sharing the stories in this book serves to confirm its premise, which is that every married man in America has a wife who thinks he is an idiot. In fact, it proves to be even more universal a phenomenon than I expected. In interviews and book signings all across the land, North and South, East and West, I came to the inescapable conclusion that there are two kinds of wives in this country: the ones who think their husbands are idiots, and the ones who are lying to you about it.

If you are a married woman reading this right now, I ask you: Do you think your husband is an idiot? If your answer is no, my response is: Oh yes you do. Or, maybe you are a married man and you are thinking: *My wife doesn't think I'm an idiot.* Pal, I hate to break it to you, but yes she does. And the fact that you don't realize it probably proves she's right.

Anyway, I guess you would say I was humbled, or humiliated, on the date of publication of this book, and then I was humbled, again and again, as I traveled across this country promoting it. I'll never forget those three months. I'll never forget the line that stretched around the block and out of sight in Columbus, Ohio. I'll never forget the security guards who let us keep a mall in Dallas open an extra half hour so everybody could get their books signed. I'll never forget Golic showing up with me at so many of the appearances, and scribbling his name over my signature in hundreds of books. I'll never forget the manager of the bookstore in Washington, D.C., telling me: "We didn't get this many people for Laura Bush." I'll never forget the reception at my signing in Connecticut, when I found out I had made the *New York Times* bestseller list.

I'll also never forget the kindness of all the media escorts who showed me around cities, big and small, that I might never otherwise have visited. And most of all, I'll always cherish the memory of the thousands of people who came out to see me at thirty-one signings in twenty-six cities. *You* made this a once-in-a-lifetime experience for me. It was my dream, and in the end it was everything I ever hoped it would be.

Contents

PROLOGUE
Confessions of a Metrosexual Sportscaster

I HAVE BEEN A METROSEXUAL since long before there was such a word.

I like Prada and Gucci, facials and manicures. I exfoliate, I moisturize, I know what the hot color is for this season. I know you never put cuffs on corduroy pants or mix polka dots and stripes. I have my hair cut by a stylist, not a barber, and my monthly dry-cleaning bill probably exceeds the gross national product of several small island nations.

You would probably say I am a textbook metrosexual, but that is not all I am.

I am also a professional sportscaster.

I have been covering sports for sixteen years. I covered Michael Jordan's championship teams. I have interviewed Wayne Gretzky, Roger Clemens, and Joe Montana. I have been to Super Bowls and World Series, All-Star Games and Final Fours. I know more football than any truck driver, more baseball than any fantasy geek, more hoops than any baller on the playground. I grew up worshipping Joe Namath and Walt Frazier, the first metrosexual athletes; there have been plenty more since then, but I believe I am a first.

I am a metrosexual sportscaster.

I know Hermès and hockey. I like football and foie gras. I appreciate Zegna ties and infield flies. I can tell you which wine to order with Kobe beef and how many points Kobe Bryant scored. I love the way cashmere feels and I love the way Yankee Stadium smells. My favorite meals in Chicago are steaks at Gibson's and hot dogs at Wrigley. I respect the flamboyance of Betsey Johnson and the showmanship of Magic Johnson. I admire Ralph Lauren and Ralph Sampson. I know Salvatore Ferragamo and Vince Ferragamo, Roberto Cavalli and Roberto Clemente, Nicole Miller and Reggie Miller, *and* I know that Christian Lacroix is a fashion designer from Paris, not a third-line right winger from Moose Jaw, Saskatchewan.

So, that is what I am. But it is not *who* I am. In every other way, I am just like you. A guy with a family and a lot of responsibilities and a lot of angst. Hosting the number one morning sports talk show in America doesn't remove angst; mostly it creates it. Just because millions of people listen to me every day doesn't mean my life is easy, and it certainly doesn't mean people treat me differently than they treat you. Assuming they treat you like an irrelevant schmuck.

That's the point: You and I are mostly the same. We work too hard and laugh too loudly. We sleep too little and eat too much. We do our best to balance our lives: racing out of meetings to make it to soccer games, flying home on red-eyes for Saturday music classes, getting chiropractic adjustments for carrying three-year-olds. Some days we feel like life is a train and we're chasing it, and there are days when the train is getting away from us, into the distance.

There were three times in my life when those feelings threatened to overwhelm me. When, despite all my blessings, I could not escape the feeling of impending doom. During those times I turned to a psychiatrist for help. (I've done that also in the best of times, by the way. And, just for the record, it has been my experience that therapy is much more fun when you're happy.) When I became especially agitated, Dr. Gray suggested I keep a journal, a diary. She recommended I keep track of my feelings daily, or as often as I could, in order to make sense of them.

"Michael," she told me, "reading the way you express your feelings will make you understand them in a way you never imagined possible."

So, what follows are selected entries from my journal, written from my front-row seat at this grand opera we call life, over the months and years it has taken for me to no longer need to write them. I did it because my shrink said it would help me become a better parent and a better husband, a better sportscaster and a better man.

God, I hope she was right.

FIRST TRIP
to the Supermarket

June 1999 – February 2000

The First Trimester: **Denial**

I MUST CONFESS, the very first thought that went through my mind was that Ricky Ricardo was full of shit. And that devastates me, because I love Ricky Ricardo. The man was wearing clothes in the fifties that would still be hip today, and he made smoking look so cool I started doing it. To my mind, he was the coolest character in the history of television.

What a shame he was so obviously full of shit.

I'll tell you how I know: Remember the episode where Lucy tells Ricky she's pregnant? She does it anonymously, making him figure it out in front of his audience at the Tropicana nightclub. Ricky sings "We're Having a Baby, My Baby and Me," trying to guess which guest is the lucky one. Do you remember how he strolls right past Lucy without the *foggiest* notion it might be she who is expecting? What are we to make of this? Was it the second Immaculate Conception? Had Ricky *never* traversed the space between those separated twin beds? Could it really have been that much of a surprise?

Now, this was the fifties, so I'm willing to cut them slack on sexual chemistry. I suppose in the time of Joseph McCarthy, network censors might have been squeamish if Lucy had said, "I should go off the Ortho-Cept this week. Last time it took me three months to get my period."

But did they really need to insult our intelligence?

Now, maybe it was better the way they did it. I certainly didn't need to hear Lucy tell Ricky she was ovulating, or tell Ethel she was three centimeters dilated and twenty percent effaced. I don't regret never seeing Lucille Ball in the stirrups, or bored out of her mind on bed rest because she was carrying too low and they didn't want to use a stitch in her cervix. Perhaps the world was a better place when we were spared all of that on television, but mustn't Ricky have had *some* inkling that Lucy might be knocked up?

The point of all this is that today, my wife told me we are going to have a baby. Unlike Ricky, I was not shocked by the news. Not after we went off the pill three months ago, visited three obstetricians and a pediatrician, pinpointed the optimal instant of ovulation, became unprecedentedly intimate with a thermometer, had sex when I didn't feel like it (a first), and spent hundreds of dollars on books— everything from prenatal diet tips to the benefits of communication with the fetus. Like everything else in my life, this transaction was carefully budgeted, programmed by a computer, dissected on a spreadsheet, discussed via e-mail, and scheduled in my BlackBerry long before any rabbit died. My wife didn't need to slip me an anonymous note, and there was no point in feigning surprise. This was a day that was only about the facts.

We're having a baby. My baby and me.

The first thing I have learned is that my role in all of this is negligible. My wife's obstetrician made that abundantly clear when I made the catastrophic mistake of attending an appointment. What I found is that my contribution to anything beyond insemination is purely optional. There was not a single question I asked to which the reply was not: It doesn't matter.

Should I exercise more?

Should I stop smoking?

Should I get more sleep?

Is there anything I should do about my diet?

It doesn't matter.

But the doctor *did* have a great deal to say to my wife and, frankly, the language she used was absurd. Am I really supposed to know what a uterus is? I mean, does everyone?

Apparently my wife thinks they do.

"How in the world can you not know what a uterus is?" she asked.

"Well," I said, "I don't have one."

"You don't have a satellite dish, either. But you know what that is."

"Do you know what rack-and-pinion steering is?" I asked.

"No."

"Well, you see," I said, "I don't make fun of you."

"I cannot believe you would compare rack-and-pinion steering to my uterus."

I realized there was no good end to this conversation.

"Well, does anyone want to tell me what a uterus is?" I asked.

Without blinking, the doctor pulled down a roll-up picture of a frontally nude woman with her abdominal cavity on display. And I immediately regretted not having pursued the rack-and-pinion line of questioning. By the time she finished, I needed a stiff drink.

That was how we began the horrifying process of insemination, which I must say bears absolutely no resemblance to actual sex. As Tom says to himself in *The Adventures of Tom Sawyer:* "Work consists of whatever a body is *obliged* to do. . . . Play consists of whatever a body is not obliged to do." I was stunned at how quickly sex started to seem like work when it became something my body was obliged to do.

Let's do it now, honey. Seinfeld *starts in eight minutes.*

I actually spoke those words. What has become of me?

Though, on the positive side, I will say this: There is something liberating about a sexual experience where the sole objective is to get it over with as quickly as possible. It alleviates all the pressure. And all she wants to do is get it done and then lie flat on her back with her feet in the air like a T-square, anyway. She's just as happy as you are if it's over in time for *Seinfeld.*

So eventually it happened. Three months of that and away we go. I would describe my wife's overriding emotion as relief; she has so many friends who've had trouble getting pregnant, she's behaving as though the hard part is behind us. Me, though, I feel like I'm standing on the edge of a giant cliff and cannot see what is waiting for me once I go over. There isn't a hint of euphoria or delight or even joy. All I feel is a distant but heavy sense of dread. We'll see how that changes—if it does—as time goes on.

Dr. Gray has recommended that I keep this diary for the duration of the pregnancy. I pledge to be diligent in doing so, even though I have some doubt as to how much good will come of it. I figure, if nothing else, maybe it will make for interesting reading someday.

Note to self: At some point, make sure you write a letter to unborn child. A tad kitschy, perhaps, but an idea I find appealing. Perhaps I'll read it at the kid's wedding someday and everyone will cry at the majesty of it. Be sure to write it majestically.

● ● ● ●

Just back from a visit with Dr. Gray, who has the uncanny ability to be uplifting while she explains that I am doomed to forever be unhappy.

"What you must come to accept," she told me, "is that we all have priorities in life. Those priorities define who we are, and yours are about to change."

"But what if they don't change?" I asked. "I am the most self-centered person on earth. What if I remain that way even after the baby is born?"

"It does not happen that way, Michael," she said, "not for us who love our children and put them first."

That's the trouble. Sometimes you don't put the really important things first. I should know; I talk about sports for a living.

"Ah, yes," she said, "the games you enjoy so well."

"I do enjoy them, but it's more than that."

"How so?"

I thought about it for a minute. "I don't know."

"Think about it," she said. "If you can tell me why you love sports so much, it may give us the answers to other questions, too."

Well, I spent the rest of the day thinking about it.

I love the fact that my father, a man who grew up penniless during the Depression, refers to the Yankees' loss of a World Series game as the worst moment of his childhood. And I love that after making himself a successful lawyer and publishing a book, he dedicated it to his heroes, including Joe DiMaggio along with Clarence Darrow and William O. Douglas.

I love the fact that my mother, who grew up within walking distance of Yankee Stadium, is such a passionate sports fan herself that she must watch games alone because she finds conversation distracting. And I love that she would have left my father for Joe Namath in a heartbeat, and that he would have applauded her for it.

I love that my kid brother, who—like all kid brothers—always hated everything I liked, chose to root for the Miami Dolphins because they were the sworn enemy of my beloved New York Jets. And I love that, thirty years later, he flies to Miami every time the Dolphins have a big game.

I love that my wife, who grew up without sports playing any role in her life, now watches games with me and occasionally puts down her magazine. I love that she recognizes it is important enough at least to try.

I love the way I felt the first time I covered the Super Bowl. It was Pasadena, California, in January 1993. The Bills were playing the Cowboys and Garth Brooks sang the national anthem. I remember thinking about all the games I'd watched as a kid, and how if someone had told that kid he would someday get to cover the Super Bowl he would have said, "I am going to have the best life of anybody in the whole world." And then U.S. Navy jets flew overhead in formation just as the sun set over the mountains in the distance. That stadium was the loudest place I've ever been.

I love that Dave Wannstedt, then the coach of the Chicago Bears, once yelled at me over something I'd said on the radio, and I stumbled into the pressroom, humiliated, and a veteran writer pulled me aside and said, "Don't sweat it, kid. They never yell unless they know you're right."

I love the way Michael Jordan used to pump his fist when he made a big shot. I love the way Pete Rose ran to first base when he could have walked. I love that Lou Gehrig really believed he was the luckiest man on the face of the earth.

There are so many things to love about sports, so many moments and thrills. But, as I think about it, none of those really have anything to do with the question. Those are not the reasons I love sports. They are symptoms; the question is about the disease.

Upon further reflection, I have decided that what I *really* love most about sports is the impermanence. Sports are like war without all the dying. Imagine how intriguing war would be as a spectator sport if, when it was over, everyone shook hands and showered together. The strategy, the passion, the courage, the stakes; war is magnificent theater until you start counting bodies. That's where you lose me.

In sports, you never lose me. You plan your attack, prepare physically and emotionally, attempt to execute your game plan—often in hostile environments—and then it ends and you all have a beer together.

That is the beauty of sports. That is the reason I became a sportscaster in the first place, because of the impermanence.

You see, growing up I wanted to be a journalist—a *real* journalist. I wanted to cover politics and uncover corruption and ask the questions that topple the high and mighty. But all that changed when Andrew Donatelli drowned.

I never met Donatelli, but I'll never forget him. A high school senior in a small town where I was doing an internship at the local newspaper, the kid was headed to college on a football scholarship and was valedictorian of his high school class. He also had the prettiest girlfriend you could imagine and the saddest dog I ever saw. The night of his prom, Donatelli and a few buddies took their dates to a beach; some were drinking beer and others were allegedly smoking pot. Somehow that pretty girlfriend wound up in the water and Donatelli inexplicably drowned saving her. The next morning, the newspaper sent three of us on the story, one to the police station, one to the beach, and one—me—to the house to interview the parents.

I went. I stood on the porch. That was where I saw the dog. He came around the house from the backyard and stared at me. The dog was handsome but powerful looking, like a guard dog. I don't suppose there were many times a stranger could have stood on that porch without the dog barking, but this wasn't the day for that. He just watched me for a little while and then grew bored and flopped to the ground with his back to me. He didn't move after that, not in all the time I stood on that porch, which had to be an hour. I've never seen a dog so still. He wasn't asleep, either, just sad. Dogs may not understand everything, but they usually know when to be sad.

I couldn't ring the bell.

I had all my questions written in my yellow reporter's pad but I couldn't ask them; I knew it was my job but I just couldn't. I couldn't ask a woman I'd never met how it felt to go to Malcolm and Brothers Funeral Home on Worth Avenue at five in the morning with a football uniform and a navy blue Brooks Brothers suit because she couldn't decide which her son would have wanted to be buried in. I have all the respect in the world for people who ask that question, but I can't.

The experience really shook me up. It also made me wonder, for the first time, what I would do with my life. I had always wanted to be a journalist; now I would have to be something else. I told that to my adviser, in those words exactly.

"Have you ever thought about covering sports?" he said.

Funny that he barely knew me and still asked that.

So that is the story of how I became a sportscaster, and it is also the best way I can think of to explain why I love sports so much. There is nothing in the world better than investing everything into something that means absolutely nothing.

I often read about people whose lives are filled with tragedy, civil war, poverty, hunger, and I think how much better off the world would be if everyone could spend all that energy worrying about football. Maybe I'm onto something with that. Maybe the solution to all our problems can be found in irrelevance. Try it. The next time the mortgage is due and the baby is crying and you're late for work and the car in front of you is taking up both lanes—that is the *best* time to fret over someone dropping a ball you care too much about. It may not make your troubles disappear but it might make them blurry, distort the focus, at least a little. Maybe, on a tough day, that is the most we can ask for. Maybe that's what I should be passing along to my child someday. Maybe the best thing any of us can wish for is just a little blurriness.

• • •

There is nothing at all blurry about the way I feel today. The word of the day is *anxious* and my anxiety is not at all blurry; it is crystal clear. I've felt this way since the phone rang too early this morning, and my feelings of anxiety have only grown as the day has worn on. It has reached the point where I am so anxious I can hardly sit still. In keeping with the intention of this journal, I am writing in hope that trying to explain the events of the day will relax me.

It was my Aunt Ada who woke us up this morning, on a bad phone line. It sounded like she was calling from a cell phone in the Brazilian rain forest. When she told me she was on an airplane my heart started to race. Why would my aunt be calling from an airplane?

"Darling," she said, in her whiny soprano, "grab a pencil."

"All right."

"Take down these numbers. Three, nine, twenty-two, forty-six, fifty-five, and sixty-one."

She was shouting; I can only imagine how loud it must have been if you were seated beside her.

"Those are the numbers on my lotto ticket," she said. "I put the ticket in the freezer, under the mushroom barley."

"What?"

"I didn't make the soup, darling. It's Tabatchnick."

"Aunt Ada, why are you telling me this?"

"In case the plane crashes," she said. "I share the tickets with the girls from mahjong, and if I go down they'll never cut the family in on my share!"

I looked at the clock. It was five in the morning.

"Aunt Ada, do you know what time it is?"

"What am I, blind?" she asked, in the way that every member of my family answers questions with questions. "I'm on the red-eye to Vegas."

My father's sister was widowed young. She has no children, but she does have a bit of a gambling problem. For instance, she always spends the week of the Super Bowl in Las Vegas so she can make every prop wager known to man. (Last year she made me ask my research department to do a study on the history of the coin toss.)

"Have you got the numbers, darling?" she asked.

"I have them, Aunt Ada."

"All right, go back to sleep. If you wake up to terrible news, make sure you watch the lotto tonight."

I hung up and sat bolt upright in bed, which awoke my pregnant wife. Somehow she had managed to sleep through the entire conversation, but my sitting up woke her.

"What the hell is going on?" she asked.

"It's nothing, honey," I told her. "Go back to sleep."

She shook her head in that way that means she's aggravated. Then she fell back to sleep. Watching her, I wanted to cry. She's a wonderful woman and now she's only months away from giving birth to a child whose blood is catastrophically tainted by the dementia of my family. I laid my head down but knew I would not sleep. I could not stop thinking about the baby. What chance does it have for a normal life? What chance could *anyone* have in this lunatic family where they call at five in the morning just in case they win the lottery and die in a plane crash on the same day?

Such is the curse my child is being born into, a tragedy of Shakespearean proportions. It reminds me of the line at the beginning of *Angela's Ashes*, where Frank McCourt says there is nothing as miserable as an impoverished Irish childhood. He would change his mind in a hurry if he ever spent Thanksgiving with my family.

That's how my day began. I assumed the pit in my stomach would fade, but as the hours passed, just the opposite happened. My sense of impending doom only grew. After lunch I decided it might cheer me up to call my parents in Palm Beach and give them the big news. What I forgot is that calling my parents has really never cheered up anyone.

My mother answered the phone and immediately started yelling at my father.

"Come here, you aren't going to believe this!"

I could hear him in the distance. "What the hell do you want?"

"Just come in here a minute!"

"What is so important it can't wait five minutes for a commercial?"

"Is this man unbelievable?" she asked into the phone. "He's watching the Marx Brothers, what could he possibly miss?"

"You don't have to disturb him," I started to say, but she was already shouting.

"Is it too much to ask to have you come here when I say it's important?"

"For forty-one years it's been important! I can't do anything without you needing me for something important!"

"Then leave, why don't you? If it's so hard to be with me, just leave already!"

"I'm going! I'm going!"

For forty-one years, he's been going.

"Are you coming in here or what?" she shouted.

"What the hell is so important?"

"It's the telephone!"

"Who is it?"

"It's Fred Astaire, he wants to give you dance lessons. Can't you just trust if I say it's important?"

"For forty-one years it's been important. That's why I've never seen the end of a movie!"

It was around that point that I hung up. The pit is still gnawing at my stomach; it feels like a hamster running on a wheel. I still feel anxious. And, it occurs to me, I'm going to have to call another time to give my father the news.

*   *   *

She'll never wear the green shoes.

That's how well I know her.

Which isn't to say I understand her; I certainly do not *understand* her but I *know* her, and I know there isn't any way in hell she's going to come out of that closet wearing the green shoes.

I should explain that my wife wears black like a suit of armor. It is her protection, her only color, and now she is convinced that the only reason her cousin asked her to be a bridesmaid is so she would have to wear a lime-green dress.

"I mean just *look* at it," she shrieked when she brought it home, still wrapped in cellophane. "Barbara Bush wouldn't wear this!"

Tonight, she emerged from her closet wearing the dress and a pair of lime-green shoes which, she told me, had been recommended by the bride.

"That's the part that really gets me," she said. "She doesn't *insist* you wear these horrendous shoes, she just *recommends* it. So you're a bitch if you don't but you can't complain because she didn't *make* you wear them."

She was teetering dangerously close to that place where anger turns to tears, which is a bad place to be when we are due in Fairfield, Connecticut, in two hours and the traffic on the parkway is guaranteed to be a nightmare.

"You know what?" I said, as gently as I could. "I think they look great."

She gave me a look that said: *How could I have married someone with as little sense as you have?*

But I hung tough. "I know it isn't your style, but it's actually a nice look, especially with your hair up like that. You're only having trouble with it because it's so different from what you usually wear."

She softened. I was getting to her.

"I'll be waiting downstairs," I said. "You do whatever you want, but I think the shoes look great."

I left her staring at her feet. Now it's been forty minutes and we are guaranteed to be late to this wedding, which will create endless strife in the family. Our tardiness is sure to be the topic of conversation at holiday gatherings for twenty years, but she's still up there struggling with the shoes. I'll say one thing: If she comes down wearing the green ones, then there is more power in hormones than there is in an atomic bomb, because under normal circumstances there is no way I could convince her to make even an insignificant change in her life, much less something as enormous as wearing green shoes.

I hear her coming. I'll let you know what happened.

The following day

What a horror show *that* proved to be.

It began before we even left, when a moth flew in. We both saw it go past us into the living room and disappear near a light fixture. Now, I hate moths but I must say this did not cause me nearly the consternation it did my wife. Before I could stop her she had kicked off her *black* shoes and climbed up on a kitchen stool, swinging a broom over her head. Mind you, we were now inside of an hour from the time we were supposed to be at this wedding.

The notion flashed through my mind that the pregnancy was making her delusional. "Honey," I said, "this hardly seems worth the trouble."

"We have to get rid of it!" she shouted, swinging the broom like Derek Jeter.

"It's a *moth*," I said. "Are you worried it's going to steal the television?"

Well, as it turned out we were a good half hour late to the wedding, my wife refused to wear any shoes at all during the ceremony, the best man made a drunken toast in which he reminisced too fondly about the groom's womanizing, and I got a speeding ticket on the way home because my wife had to pee really badly.

Oh, and the moth lived.

Then I was in bed, just on the verge of falling asleep, when I heard her burst into the room, crying loudly. (I should mention that my wife cries every time she sees the movie *Rudy*, so upon hearing her cry I was not panicked.)

"I'm bleeding all over the place!" she shouted.

That is when I panicked.

It turns out she had been in the kitchen and opened a cupboard, then bent to pick something up and cracked her head when she stood. I got dressed as quickly as I could and raced her to the emergency room, where we were seated amid a collection of gunshot-wound victims. She had a bathing cap filled with ice cubes against her head.

"Honey, are you feeling faint?" I asked.

"I didn't want to bleed on my new Burberry," she said.

She was wearing *my* raincoat.

It was almost two hours before they called us in to see a doctor. There were two other patients in the room where they took us: a woman who looked as though she had been stabbed in the ribs, and a man with bandages covering his entire head. I later found out he had fallen off his motorcycle and skidded almost fifty yards on his face. A nurse told me she'd be surprised if he didn't need skin grafts on over seventy-five percent of his body. Nothing like skin grafts to put things in perspective.

Then the doctor came in carrying a needle that must have been nine inches long. I thought I would pass out; if he had actually stuck that needle into my wife's head, it would have come out beneath her jaw. I could not say a word, even good-bye, until the doctor squeezed the top and I realized it was just a syringe filled with water to clean the cut. My relief was probably evident on my face, though no one would have noticed because when that water struck my wife's head, all eyes in the room turned to her.

"MOTHERFUCKER!"

All the action stopped. Even the guy who had lost half his face on I-95 turned to see where that sound had come from.

"That hurts," she said, more softly.

It wasn't long before the subject of stitches was raised. The doctor said she would need between seven and nine. Then the subject of shaving the head was raised.

"We could shave such a small area I doubt anyone would even notice," the doctor said.

Doc, meet my wife.

"There is *no chance* we are shaving *any* of my head," she said. "There has to be another option."

"There is," the doctor said hesitantly, "but it isn't as desirable. We can staple the wound. It isn't what I would advise, but it will work. You'll come back in a week and we can take the staple out."

"And I won't lose any hair?" she asked.

"You won't lose any hair."

"Then that's what I want."

I felt I had to say something. "Doctor, are you sure this is an effective medical solution to the problem?"

My wife gave me a look that said when we got home I was getting kicked in the nuts.

"It is safe and effective," the doctor said. "It's more commonly performed on the homeless and others without medical insurance, but it's not dangerous."

"We're doing it," my wife said. "Get the stapler."

And that's exactly what the doctor got. With one quick motion, he stapled my wife's head like a term paper.

Thwack!

She's asleep upstairs now. If you catch it at exactly the right angle, the staple gleams in the light. She'll be fine; she always is. Come to think of it, I may be giving a false and completely unfair impression of this woman. She is an intelligent and accomplished corporate executive and I am enormously proud of her. (When we were first married, she made more money than me and people asked how I handled that. I bought a BMW, that's how I handled it. All men should be cursed with a wife who makes a six-figure salary.)

And I suppose that while we're on the subject of my wife, I should tell you that shoes are her reason for being. They are her passion, her raison d'être. My wife has more shoes than Imelda Marcos. And they all look more or less alike, which I suppose is why she always has such a difficult time deciding which ones to wear.

A typical evening for us will begin with my wife repeating over and over the time by which I need to be ready to leave the house. When that time comes I invariably find myself sitting on the sofa, shaved, showered, and dressed and shouting time checks at three-minute intervals while she scurries about madly wearing two unmatched shoes.

Then disaster strikes.

She always asks me which shoe I like better. This is unfair. While I am familiar with Jimmy Choo and Manolo Blahnik, that doesn't mean I can tell them apart. Half the time, I'm not even certain they aren't a matching pair.

Then it gets worse.

After I choose which of the identical shoes I prefer, she asks why.

Now, I don't have a compelling reason for almost *anything* I do. I spend my life wandering about in a state of total indifference, so I certainly don't have a convincing reason why I prefer one black strappy sandal over another. This inability on my part invariably makes us even later.

Of course, I hope it is clear that I say all of this with love. If she didn't recognize the importance of these shoes, who would? I'm glad someone does, and I'm glad that someone is married to me. And now, as I watch her sleep, with an industrial-sized office supply embedded in her scalp, I am reminded of just how sincerely I mean that. As crazy as it seems, I love her more every time we have that fight.

. . .

I had a funny experience last night.

Actually, maybe it wasn't really funny as much as it was sad.

You be the judge. It was around ten o'clock and I was bushed. I mean, *really* tired. The kind of tired where Charlize Theron could be beside you in bed with a jug of wine and a tray of grapes and all you would say to her would be "If you're going to read, please be mindful of how loudly you turn the pages."

I fell into bed and let out an audible sigh—more of a moan, actually—then rolled over, picked up the phone, and dialed zero.

"I need a wake-up call at four o'clock, please," I said.

There was a pause. "Excuse me?"

"I know it's early, but that's when I get up."

"Sir, I don't know what you're talking about."

Then it hit me. I wasn't in a hotel. This was my home. I was talking to a regular operator. I hung up and set my alarm clock, then started to laugh. I've definitely been traveling too much.

This was not the first time something like that has happened. In fact, back when I was on the road *all* the time—covering teams—I used to play a game when I woke up: I would see if I could remember what city I was in before I opened my eyes.

All of us who work too much have had those sorts of experiences, like dialing nine for an outside line from our home phone. For me, though, it has always been worth it. I have lived my dream and loved every minute of it. I wouldn't part with any of the experiences I've had, not for anything.

Like the time I sat with Muhammad Ali in a hospitality room in Atlanta and listened to him talk about watching Mike Tyson fight.

Or that morning in New Orleans when Paul Prudhomme, the legendary chef, cooked me breakfast. He made omelets with sweet potatoes and spicy sausage and let me eat right out of his frying pan, and wash it down with fresh coffee with chicory. Nothing has ever tasted better, not in my whole life.

Or the time Mark McGwire handed me his bat at the All-Star Game in San Diego so he could use my cell phone to do a guest appearance on a radio show.

Or the afternoon I spent with O. J. Simpson, who complimented me on my tie while he chatted up an awestruck blonde, six months before his ex-wife was murdered.

Or being ten feet away from Larry Holmes when he threw up in the ring after going the distance with Evander Holyfield.

Or that night when the Reverend Jesse Jackson tapped me on the shoulder and introduced himself in the old Chicago Stadium. He said he wanted to go on the air and talk about the Bulls. And he did and he was wonderful, and knew more about basketball than most of the reporters covering the game.

I've had mayors in three cities proclaim days in my honor, I've interviewed Woody Allen and Jack Nicholson, the governor of Illinois calls me "Greeny," and I once convinced Senator Joseph Lieberman to do an impression of Sylvester Stallone on the air. The only thing more amazing than any of those is that I got paid for all of them. It almost doesn't seem fair.

So here's the question now: Is it all going to have to end?

It might. When I was growing up, I don't think I would have wanted *my* dad on the road two hundred days a year. I don't think I would have liked seeing him more on television than I did in person. I don't think I would have been excited to hear about his dinner at the White House; I would have wanted him to eat at *my* house, with me. I suppose that means I'm going to have to start eating at home. That's going to take some getting used to.

Now, I *can* see where there is going to be a bright side to this crazy job of mine. Maybe my kids will come with me to the Super Bowl someday. Maybe I'll bring them on the field before the game, and into the locker rooms to meet all the players. My kids will be the coolest ones in school if I do that. (When I was ten, the girl in my class who picked her nose took me to a World Series game. She was my best friend for the rest of the year.)

That's going to be great, but it's a long way off. And between now and then, I'm going to have to be there. Not in Miami, not in Atlanta, not in L.A.

There.

Which, I suppose, is now forever to be defined as "wherever the kid is."

I guess this means I am going to have to put something ahead of sports. And ahead of myself. That's going to be quite an adjustment. Frankly, I wouldn't bet I'll be able to make it.

The Second Trimester: **Acceptance**

WELL, I'VE GOT good news and bad news.

The good news is, I was able to make my dad awfully happy. Today I told him he is going to be a grandfather. I told him over breakfast, which we ate together at my house. (He's in town for the start of the New York Jets' season; he always flies in for the opening game.)

My wife and I told him the news while he was taking a bite of a bialy, and he got excited and the butter and jam got all over his face. Then it got all over our faces too when he hugged and kissed us.

That was wonderful.

Then we went to the football game.

I won't belabor this because it is just too painful. In the second quarter, the Jets' most important player, the quarterback Vinny Testaverde, blew out his Achilles tendon. He is done for the year. This was the very first game of a very promising season, and just like that it is all over. The team is doomed.

When the game was over, my dad and I just sat there, crushed. Then my father spoke, bringing the perspective that comes only with maturity and experience.

"I think I'm going to throw up."

I nodded.

He said: "We have to remember that you're going to have a baby. That's the most important thing."

"Of course it is," I agreed. "But I was really looking forward to this year. I really thought we were finally going to the Super Bowl."

"It's just not meant to happen," he said. "We're cursed. The whole franchise operates under a dark cloud."

We sat in silence a few minutes, watching the other fans file out slowly. Every head was down.

"Of course, the most important thing is the baby," my dad said.

"Of course."

The stadium was almost empty, but we didn't move. There wasn't anywhere to go. Not until the following season, anyway.

"I'm giving up these tickets," my father said. "I live a thousand miles away. I make myself crazy every week, trying to decide if I should come up here, freeze my ass off in December, and all they do is break my heart. It's ridiculous!"

"I know," I said. "I'm so aggravated I could bite through the foam finger that guy dropped over there."

"It's a tragedy, Michael. It's like we're being punished for something."

The cleanup crew was closing in on us now, blowing hot dog wrappers and paper cups into the air with giant vacuums that roared like airplanes taking off.

"I think I *will* come to the game next week," my father said. "But if they lose, that's it. I'm never coming to another game as long as I live."

I couldn't blame him.

"Of course," he said, "the most important thing is the baby."

"Of course it is."

Then we left. The drive home seemed to take longer than usual. When we arrived my wife was holding a bottle of champagne. She had no intention of drinking any; she's pregnant now. She won't be drinking for a while. The champagne was for my dad and me. But just then we didn't feel like it.

"Come on, you two," she said. "Isn't the baby more important than a football game?"

My dad and I looked at each other and answered in perfect unison. "Of course it is."

But we didn't drink any of the champagne. It's in the refrigerator. I assume I'll feel like drinking it someday.

●　　●　　●

I drank a whole lot of champagne last night. Not the stuff from my fridge; this was wedding champagne. Good stuff, too. Perrier-Jouët, Grand Brut. (I didn't get the year, but no matter—those are top-of-the-line bubbles.)

So maybe it was the champagne. Or maybe it was the tension I've been feeling lately. (This was the first time I'd been drunk since we got pregnant.) But whatever the excuse, the reality is that I humiliated myself in a way only I can.

What a shame, too, because the evening began so well. First, the champagne was available before the ceremony; that's solid. It makes a longer service much easier to sit through. Add to that the fact that the bride is among my wife's closest friends, so they were off together all afternoon, leaving me to my own devices, which meant golf during the day and too much champagne before the ceremony.

By the time everyone moved on to the cocktail hour, I had moved into another dimension. I was in a wonderful mood, mostly because the particular drunk you get from champagne is my favorite. There is something jubilant in the aftertaste, something very cheerful in the carbonation. If laughter had a taste, it would taste like champagne. Or, if all the various forms of liquor were rooms in a house, champagne would be the great room, where you do all your entertaining. (By contrast, vodka would be the bedroom, bourbon the basement, gin the attic, and beer that room downstairs with the pool table where your buddy puked once and it's never smelled right since.)

So I was buzzing and holding court, which is the best part of being a little famous: You get to hold court at other people's weddings. And I'm usually pretty good at it. In this case, I was cracking up a room full of sports fans while they ignored angry stares from their wives. (It has been my experience that no one ever walks away from stories about pickup games with Michael Jordan.)

Just when I had the room really shaking, a strange woman walked in. She looked confused. She also looked like a hooker. This was a fancy, black-tie affair, but this woman looked like she'd have been right at home leaning against a streetlamp at midnight.

Well, I guess I was caught up in the revelry, because too loudly I said to the fellows, "I'm glad to see the hooker got here!"

Silence.

It was astounding how quiet the room became, all of a sudden. And I couldn't decide how many people had heard it. Maybe everyone had. Maybe the hooker had, I couldn't tell; she disappeared from sight as quickly as she'd come in. I wasn't sure if she'd left or just blended with the crowd. In moments like those, I invariably break out in the sort of sweat Albert Brooks showed off in *Broadcast News*. So there I was, soaking a Calvin Klein tux from the inside, when I saw another late arrival. A man this time, and he looked familiar.

"Keith?"

It was my old college roommate. I hadn't seen him in ten years, hadn't spoken to him in five. We'd lost touch after he moved out of the country on a business venture. I'm pretty sure he went to Prague, though it may have been Paris. Or Peking. I forget.

"You look great," I told him.

"You too," he said. "Congratulations on the show. I listen every morning."

"You're back in the States?"

"I am," he said. "I've been back about two years."

"That's terrific."

"I'd love to meet your wife," he said. "I hear you talk about her all the time. Is she here?"

"She is," I said, scanning the crowd for her. "How about you, are you married?"

"I am," he said. "Two months. We just got back from our honeymoon."

"Wow, newlyweds. That's great. Is she here?"

"I think so," he said, looking around. "She's supposed to meet me."

I assume you can see where this is going. He was married to the hooker. Though, to be fair, I should point out that she wasn't actually a hooker.

I'll say this: If she *did* hear what I said, she's one hell of a sport, because she never let on, not through the whole evening. But lest you worry that justice was not served, you can rest assured that my evening was ruined. I spent the entire night waiting for my old buddy to say, "So, you think my wife looks like a hooker?"

That was my penance.

Thankfully, it never happened. In fact, my own wife didn't even find out about it until we were in the cab. I usually gauge just how stupidly I have behaved by her reaction. If she laughs, it means it wasn't that serious.

She didn't laugh.

"I guess that's the sort of thing that could only happen to me," I said.

"I guess it is," she said, with her arms folded and no hint of a smile.

It's amazing how different that sounded when it came from her. But I guess she's right. For a guy who makes his living knowing the right things to say, it is hard to believe how often I say precisely the *wrong* thing when the microphones are off.

•   •   •

When I got off the air this morning my producer told me there was an urgent call from my aunt. There was a time when an urgent call from a woman in her seventies would have me jumping for a phone, but with Aunt Ada I have come to learn that *emergency* is a totally relative term. I called within the hour from my cell in the car.

"What, you're too busy to call me back?"

"Aunt Ada, this was the soonest I could get to a phone."

"They don't have phones where you work?"

"What can I do for you, Aunt Ada?"

"You were right on about Peyton Manning this morning—that fumble cost me a hundred bucks."

"Thank you, Aunt Ada. Now, what did you need?"

"What, I can't just call to say hello to my favorite nephew?"

"Ada, please."

"All right, darling. You're so impatient, just like your father. And by the way, you're starting to lose your hair in just the same spot he did, right where you part it. You need to move the part over a little. Don't they have people to tell you that stuff?"

"No, Ada, they have people to tell me my aunt needs to speak with me and it's urgent."

"All right, for God's sake. You'll be happy to know I was calling to pay you a compliment."

"Okay."

"This morning I found odds on Sportsbook-dot-com about the baby's sex. They have it six-to-five that you're having a boy."

"I cannot believe they have odds on the sex of my baby."

"Believe it," she said. "When's the amnio?"

"What?"

"The amnio, when's the amnio?" she said. "Are you having trouble with your ears, darling? Your Uncle Sol developed that right around your age. He was stone-deaf by the time he was fifty."

"Terrific," I said. "We're not finding out the sex."

"Michael, darling, you said you were having an amnio."

"We are, but we aren't finding out the sex. We want it to be a surprise. I said that on the radio, didn't you hear me?"

"What, am I deaf like Uncle Sol? Of course I heard it," she said. "I just thought maybe you were bullshitting. You're sort of a bullshit artist on that show sometimes."

"Well, we're not finding out the sex."

"Michael, you're unbelievable," she said. "Do you have any idea the action I can get on this?"

"Ada, I'm not finding out the sex, it's that simple."

"Hold on, darling," she said, "I have something on the stove."

Then she was gone for a long time. I drove ten miles on a crowded two-lane highway before she picked the phone back up.

"Sorry, darling," she said. "The kreplach caught fire and set off the smoke alarm. But let me ask you this, when is the ultrasound?"

"What?" I asked. "Are you all right?"

"I'm fine, darling, I have a hankie over my mouth. When is the ultrasound?"

"Next week."

"Listen to me carefully, darling," she said. "The girls from mah-jong told me a heart rate over one-fifty means a girl."

"Well, we're having it next week."

"I want you to page me from the doctor's office."

"Page you when we have the ultrasound?"

"Am I speaking Yiddish?" she asked. "Yes, page me before the news gets out."

"How is the news going to get out?"

"What, you think the doctors don't want in on the action? I guarantee you the line moves ten minutes after the news hits the street."

I was too stunned to speak.

Then she said: "I have to go, darling, the fire department is here." And she hung up.

I must remember to call and make sure she's all right.

Also, I lied to her. I don't make a habit of doing that, but in this case I believe it was justified. You see, we're actually going back to the doctor tomorrow. (It is amazing how familiar I am becoming with the hospital. It used to seem so unknowable. I think a place becomes a good deal less forbidding when you stop having to ask directions to the bathroom.) Tomorrow we will have the amniocentesis, if indeed that is how you spell it, and it wouldn't surprise me if it is not. (I'm not bothering to look it up because who cares?) To my understanding, this is the best determination we will have that the fetus is healthy. It is also the time that we *could* find out the gender of this unborn child and I, actually, would like to. (For reasons different from my aunt's.) I like to be prepared, and it only seems natural that I would gather all available information. Plus, in keeping with a more fatherly personality, I think it important that I make these types of decisions and am firm about them. That's why it is so deflating to have been vetoed so vehemently.

I have been instructed in no uncertain terms by the mother of this unborn child that to discover the gender ahead of time would render the day of delivery anticlimactic. She is quite unyielding in this belief, so much so that I have never even had the chance to make my case. So I will do it now, if only so I can say I did.

First of all, it seems to me that nothing short of an extraterrestrial invasion of our living room could possibly render the date of birth anticlimactic.

Second, and perhaps more important, I have to believe we will have so much occupying our minds on that day that a surprise will only add to the strain. I am envisioning a house filled with family and herring, my grandmother talking about her bunion surgery and my Uncle Morty saying he only eats so much at lunch so he can take his back pills. To tack any additional stress onto such a day almost seems criminal.

But I have been voted down, 1–1.

What this means is that I am destined to spend the next five months of my life as I have spent the last few, working desperately never to use a gender-specific pronoun. Every time I discuss the child I feel as though everyone is waiting for me to call it "he" or "she" so they can insist I've made a Freudian slip, that I secretly have a preference.

I tell you honestly I have no preference. In fact, I think it would be inappropriate to have one, because the implication is that there will be disappointment if it goes the other way. I feel absolutely comfortable saying that if this baby is born with a full complement of fingers and toes I will be completely satisfied. The notion that there could be the slightest hint of disappointment offends me.

In fact, I can envision pluses and minuses in either outcome.

For example, my friend Richard has two girls, and he has described for me the experience of changing their diapers in excruciating detail. What I have taken from those conversations is that every time a baby girl pees, it is imperative that you clean out the inside of her vagina.

(I pause now for an admission. It took me ten minutes to type that last word. In fact, I misspelled it twice before finally getting the little red line to disappear. It's a word I can safely say I have never used in conversation. I don't know any man who has. And if one did, I can assure you it would color my judgment of him forever. *Vagina* is even less a word than is *penis*, which is also not a word any man uses in conversation. I have never seen a guy take a knee in the wrong place, fall to the ground, and shout, "Oh! My penis!" It simply isn't done. These are medical terms that should be employed no more often than *cranial hemorrhage*. No one gets hit in the head and says he has a cranial hemorrhage; he says, "My head is bleeding!" Only in the event of a very specific injury would he invoke the words *cranial* or *hemorrhage*. It is the same with *penis* and *vagina*. But I digress.)

If Richard is cleaning out the inside of a vagina eight or ten times a day, that strikes me as a pretty good reason to be rooting for a boy. It isn't the only reason, but it may be the best.

On the other side, of the many reasons to root for a girl I would say the biggest is the opportunity to know one from the instant of her birth. Just to see if I could figure her out. I don't understand women at all. In fact, I find the better I get to know any woman, the less I understand her. Women may become predictable as you get to know them, but that does not make them decipherable. Perhaps if I have a little girl, and know her from her very first instant, I will have half a chance of understanding what makes her tick.

Note to self: Include this stuff in letter to unborn child. I think I would like to know if my father was hoping I would be a girl. For that matter, I would like to know if my father was even aware that my mother was pregnant. Perhaps my father is a bad example. But I still think it's a good idea for the letter.

The following day

Just back from the amnio. Went great. Wife unreal. They stuck a needle directly into her stomach, about two inches below her belly button. I almost fainted. All she wanted was to know if the baby is healthy, which it seems to be. There was something very nice about the whole thing. For a self-involved woman like my wife, this was a very selfless afternoon. There is a lesson in that. I hope to figure out what it is.

Note to self: Do not call Aunt Ada with the results.

· · · ·

I should not have lied to my aunt.

Despite the purity of my intentions, I just shouldn't have. Because I consider lying a big deal. That doesn't mean I don't do it; I lie all the time. I believe everyone does. But, to me, *how* they do it is very significant.

I think there is no more accurate way of separating the people that matter in your life from the ones who do not than by dividing everyone into two groups: those you lie *with*, and those you lie *to*. For instance: I try never to lie *to* my wife, but I lie *with* her all the time. We have become quite good at lying together, actually, particularly as it applies to declining invitations. We are at a stage now where we have the excuse ready before the envelope is open. Usually we don't even have to discuss a lie; eye contact is sufficient. I like that. It must be tough to be married to someone you lie to.

So I am a big believer in the significance of lying. But, that said, the events of this afternoon serve as a reminder that nothing can make you feel like shit quite like the truth.

It happened at the deli, and it managed to ruin both my mood *and* my lunch, which is especially troubling because lunch is my favorite part of the day. It always has been. That comes from my mother, even though she never made such wonderful lunches. (In fact, quite the opposite; in grade school I couldn't trade a sandwich for a drink-to-be-named-later.) My mom was a schoolteacher, and I vividly recall that when I would visit her at lunchtime she was always in a rush. That was because—like her students—she had a very specific amount of time for lunch. Even as a little boy I realized that wasn't right. I decided at the age of seven that when I grew up, I would always be the only one to decide when I ate lunch.

So lunch is a big deal and my favorite place is Vito's, an Italian deli owned and operated by actual Italians. I love Italian food but I love it less when it's prepared by a guy named Izzy Schwartz. I like my Italian food authentic, and Vito's is a dream come true; you smell the sauce before you get off the highway. Most days, my toughest decision is what to order. Meatballs? Chicken Parmigiana? Stuffed peppers? Fresh mozzarella with tomato? My mouth is watering right now.

Today I was feeling the eggplant sub when I rolled into the parking lot. Then, as soon as I got inside, I realized something was different. It was the radio; they had it on behind the counter. It was the first time I'd ever heard my radio station in the deli. (Actually, I think it was the first time I'd heard anything in the deli. Vito's is usually like a library; I think everyone is too busy salivating to carry on a conversation.)

Then it happened.

Just as it became my turn to order—just as the words "extra sauce" were about to pass through my lips—I heard my own voice. It was the radio, of course, and I stopped to see if anyone behind the counter would say anything.

"I hate that guy."

The words were spoken with an authentic accent, as they all are behind the counter at Vito's, but there was no misunderstanding them.

And it didn't end there.

"He's so pompous," another guy said, his accent even heavier, "and so much talk about his clothes—who cares?"

"That's right," a third fellow said. "Only a woman talks that way."

It was unanimous.

"Aldo," shouted the guy taking my order, "shut that off, it's upsetting the customers." Then he looked back at me. "I'm sorry, sir, what can I get for you today?"

Now I was in a quandary.

As I saw it, I had three options:

1. I could confront them with my identity. But I quickly figured that was out of the question, because I will always be the guy who had his winter coat forcibly taken away from him in tenth grade by a girl.

2. I could storm out. But that was out of the question, because I had waited in line for fifteen minutes.

3. I could alter my voice and order my lunch. Which is what I did.

As I ate my sandwich, I was thinking that the hardest thing about having a public job is that everyone feels fully free to comment on it, particularly those who *do* know who I am. People love to tell me exactly what they think of my work. You don't get that in other jobs. My dad was an attorney. I never saw anyone come up to him and say, "That cross-examination stunk out loud! They should replace you with someone who knows what the hell he's doing!"

I get that all the time.

The first bit of negativity came years ago from a well-meaning older gentleman at a health club. I had been on television for less than a week and the last thing I needed was a viewer to tell me I was doing lousy. But he did, in the friendliest way.

"Hey, you're Greeny, right?"

I nodded.

"You do a nice job. I like listening to you on the radio."

"Thank you."

"When did you start doing TV?"

"Just recently."

"I think you should stick to radio."

"What?"

"You're very natural on radio, very funny. You look stiff on TV. Are you nervous?"

"Maybe a little."

"It shows. You're moving your hands too much and I think they have too much makeup on you. You should stick to the radio."

"Okay."

"I'm just trying to help you out," he said. "I'm a big fan."

With fans like that, who needs hate mail?

Actually, I get my fair share of that, too, mostly in the form of e-mail these days, and plenty of voice mail. I still have on tape the first really nasty voice mail I ever received. I listen to it whenever I begin to feel full of myself.

"Hey, Greenberg, I just want to tell you that I think you are a pompous, condescending jerk. You sit there on television with your phony smile and your fancy suits. You're a condescending jerk. I just thought you should know what everybody watching thinks of you. Have a nice day."

I can recite it from memory.

It is a good reminder that mine is the most subjective of professions; through whatever success I've had, that guy probably still feels the same way. And if I ever find out who he is, I'll thank him for wishing me a nice day. That last sentence always leaves me feeling that, deep inside, he actually likes me.

For most guys in my line of work, a lot of the negative feedback comes from the players and coaches we cover. But in all these years I've had only one significant confrontation and, ironically, that had nothing to do with anything I'd said on the air.

The player was Steve Buechele, a third baseman for the Chicago Cubs, and it was the summer of 1994, a month before the players began the strike that canceled the World Series. Everyone knew the strike was coming and the Cubs were terrible to boot, so the atmosphere around them that summer was depressing; no team I've ever covered seemed more eager to get a season over with.

One day, about two hours before a game, I was in the clubhouse sitting by the locker of Steve Trachsel, a much-heralded young pitcher, waiting for him to arrive for an interview. I was young and not at all well known, so I kept to myself and waited quietly by the locker. At some point, I became cognizant of Buechele staring a hole right through me.

"Is there something I can help you with?" I asked.

"Yeah," he said, sneering, "I've been watching you sitting there. You're not talking to anybody, not doing anything, you're just taking up space. We've got too many reporters in here to begin with, so why don't you get the fuck out!"

I had no idea what to do. And even if I had, I was too stunned and intimidated to have done it.

"Listen," I said, trying to keep my voice from cracking, "I don't have to explain to you what I'm doing. But since you asked, I am waiting for Steve Trachsel, who said he'd meet me here. If you have a problem with me you should tell the public relations staff, and they'll tell you that I have a credential and I have every right to be here."

"You go wait in the dugout," Buechele said. "I'll bring Trachsel out when he gets back."

"That isn't your job," I said. "Please let me do mine."

The media relations director jumped in then, a decidedly good guy who knew I had done nothing wrong.

"Do me a favor," he whispered. "Go wait in the dugout and I'll bring Trachsel out. I'm not telling you that you have to, I'm just asking a favor."

I walked out with my pride intact.

The postscript is that the Cubs won the game on a Steve Buechele home run. I didn't want to approach him afterward but, to his everlasting credit, Buechele saw me across the room and shouted over.

"You need anything from me?"

I did, of course, and went to his locker with my tape recorder. And while he never did apologize, he gave me a very good interview and shook my hand afterward. I came away thinking he was a pretty decent guy and still feel that way today.

The angriest I ever was with a ballplayer was with Jack McDowell, then of the White Sox, who was a very good pitcher and among the most intelligent people I've ever met in sports. He was, and remains, a talented guitarist and a thinker capable of ideas most athletes will never comprehend. He could also be a cranky jerk, and it was that side of him that caused me to seek revenge.

It was at the All-Star Game in Baltimore, which I was covering for a radio station in Chicago. McDowell was one of very few Chicago players in the game, and thus I spent the whole weekend chasing him about, trying to get an interview. He kept putting me off, promising to do it later. He wasn't rude but it became tiresome because I really needed the interview. Finally, after I had given up, he went out and *won* the game. Now I absolutely *had* to get the interview. But I couldn't find him. He disappeared somewhere in the locker room, and as I gathered my stuff and headed to the exit, I was disconsolate. It was my first All-Star Game and I had failed to land an interview with the winning pitcher. I was sure I would be fired.

Then a miracle happened on the elevator.

I was formulating my letter of resignation when the door opened, and—to my shock—there was McDowell, surrounded by a huge crowd.

"Jack, you have to give me that interview now. It won't take long," I said, before the door had even shut behind me.

"I can't now," he said, "we're going out. I'll catch you back in Chicago."

"But Jack, you told me all week you would do it."

"Sorry, dude."

He didn't even look at me the rest of the way.

When we reached street level I saw the sea of autograph seekers. There must have been a thousand kids racing around, trying to find their heroes. I was amused by the sight of it: Cal Ripken and Mark McGwire and Tony Gwynn, right in front of me, signing for what seemed an endless stream of kids. I looked around for McDowell but he was gone, slipping away with a cap pulled over his eyes, his friends shielding him from view. No one from the mob had recognized him. He was going to get away.

Then I got an idea.

"Hey, kid," I said, grabbing the nearest teenager and pointing, "do you see that guy over there?"

"Yeah."

"That's Jack McDowell."

Within ten seconds he was completely engulfed. There were so many kids crowded around him that I'm surprised he's not still there. And since he was no longer going anywhere, he gave me a five-minute interview while he was signing. I consider that among the greatest moments of my career.

Now, the question is: What does any of this have to do with me having a baby?

The answer: Not a friggin' thing.

What can I say? If I am supposed to write about the issues that cause me angst, well, today this is it.

Besides, what causes me greater angst is the fact I promised Dr. Gray I would write in this journal every day and now we are five months in and I've only written a handful of times. It is precisely that lack of discipline that dooms me as a parent.

I'll just say it: I feel certain I am going to be a disaster as a father. It is beyond a certainty, it is an empirical truth that can be used as a postulate for advanced mathematical theory.

If A, then B.

A = I can't so much as jot down my thoughts for two lousy minutes every night.

B = My child is certain to wind up in a bell tower someday with a semi-automatic weapon, shouting incoherently about the inequities of the capitalist system.

I really need to get my head together. This thing is just beginning and already I think I'm cracking up.

•　　•　　•

Here's another pretty good illustration of just how unique my job is: Unlike a doctor or a lawyer or a pharmacist or a cabdriver or anyone else I can think of, for four hours every day I turn into a different person. That isn't to say my radio personality is an act; you can't be a phony in my business or you'll be exposed—you always have to be yourself. But behind a microphone, you can be yourself differently than you can anywhere else. I know because I do it every day.

Today was a perfect example.

You see, I am painfully, chronically, legendarily nonconfrontational. It began early, about the age of twelve, which was—not coincidentally—when I started going to basketball games. (I'll explain that in a minute.) But today a guy yelled at me and I yelled right back. *That's* why I love radio: because if the same guy had confronted me in a restaurant, I would have snuck out through the kitchen.

It began over a comment I made about the quarterback of the Minnesota Vikings, and it ended when the caller accused me of not being a journalist.

"I know I'm not a journalist," I said, over the air. "The difference between me and most of the others is that at least I know what a journalist is. I'm not sure how many guys on the air today could pick a journalist out of a lineup."

"Well, I don't see how you can sit there every day and give your opinions about sports when you never even played," the guy said.

"Good point," I said. "Let me ask you a question: Have you ever hosted a radio show?"

"No."

"Then how can you tell me I'm doing it wrong if you've never done it?"

"I don't have to host a radio show to know you stink!" he said.

"I agree," I said. "And I don't have to play in the NFL to know that Daunte Culpepper is overrated!"

He hung up then and I took a commercial break. When I came back on the air, I had a lot more to say on the subject.

> This whole issue, in my opinion, stems from the deep-seated mistrust the American people have developed for the media. Not that I blame you. The fact is, there's a lot of bad journalism out there, mostly because most people who call themselves journalists are actually communications majors who know less about Edward R. Murrow than they do Edward Scissorhands. All they know is they want to be first. That is the tragedy of journalism today: Everyone thinks the object is to get the story first when in reality the object will always be to get the story *right*.

Then I paused, for dramatic effect. That's something you learn after a few years on the air. The key to broadcasting is knowing where to put the pauses.

> Now, if you want to get into the *real* reason people criticize the media, it is because they think we are biased. And to that, all I can say is: Of course we are. After all, what can journalism possibly be besides reality as seen through the prism of the journalist? Most people in journalism have a fundamental desire to deliver truth, but that begs the crucial question: What is truth? Life is not arithmetic, and it's not black and white; it is varying shades of gray. No matter how desperately a reporter tries to ig-

nore his biases, his instincts will always lead him to interpret what he is seeing differently than someone else might. That isn't media bias, it is the human condition. To expect anything different is unrealistic and a complete waste of time.

That was how I wrapped up the show today. I am going to save the transcript. In fact, I think I'll do that regularly as I keep this journal. Maybe I'll show all of it to the baby someday. Maybe he or she will be able to figure out what the hell I was trying to say.

Anyway, I promised I would explain why I became so nonconfrontational. That began at Madison Square Garden when I was in junior high. In those days it was easy to get a ticket to see the Knicks play, in part because the NBA wasn't so popular and also because the Knicks stank. My friends and I would buy six-dollar seats—which placed us approximately three miles from the court—and then we'd sneak down to the best seats by the end of the first quarter. (These days you have to auction off a kidney to pay for those seats.)

The player of note for the Knicks then was Bill Cartwright, who later went on to win championships with Michael Jordan in Chicago. Cartwright arrived in New York surrounded by great expectations and proceeded to live up to none of them; he was mediocre when he was healthy, and more often than not he was hurt. Consequently, he was the object of much derision from the fans, especially twelve-year-olds in expensive seats.

One night I was really giving it to him: "Cartwright, you stink! You overpaid bum!"

(I know. Heckling has come a long way since then.)

In the third quarter, an usher came around and whispered in my ear.

"Young man, I just thought you'd want to know that you are sitting next to Bill's wife."

"Bill who?"

"Bill Cartwright."

I can still see the embarrassment on her face.

I've never heckled anyone since. And I have gone out of my way to avoid conflict any way I can. That goes for every relationship I have.

Except one.

It doesn't stop me on the radio. That's why I love my job so much. I am willing to say things on the air that I never would if you met me.

•　　•　　•

Tonight I took my wife to the opening of a new art gallery and drank one too many white wines. My wife loves gallery openings but I think they are a decided bore, despite my love for art. To me, the purpose of art is to find a connection with the artist. That requires concentration, which is greatly inhibited by effeminate men in black turtlenecks gabbing incessantly about texture while society sluts try to determine which of them are straight. Really, gallery openings are much more about the galleries than the art, and seeing as I have no interest in networking a room full of bad accents, I usually find myself drinking enough that it starts not to matter.

That's when I find the humor in moments.

When they tell you life is short, they could not be more wrong. Life is long, nothing will ever be longer, and most of it is dreary and mundane. The beauty of life, if any is to be found, is in a single moment, or in thousands of them. If you're lucky you might get half a dozen in a day. Go home that night and think to yourself: I had six or seven moments today when my mind completely shut off. Then go to sleep and hope to be so fortunate again tomorrow. In the final analysis, that's all we really have to

The next morning

I'd like to apologize for the abrupt finish of the above. I was drunk last night and did not notice the battery on my laptop on the verge of dying. I barely managed to hit "save," and now I cannot remember where the hell I was going with that.

I apologize also for each and every word that made it, not only because it is superficial babble but also because even I don't know what it means. What I think I was trying to say is that if one or two funny things happened at the gallery opening last night, it made the entire thing worth enduring.

Ten hours later, I'm not sure I believe that.

It was an evening that began with a frown. That was from my wife, after she asked me which shoe I preferred and I chose the Prada heel. The frown was because she was leaning that way but my agreement caused her doubt. Then she disappeared again, and I was left to sit on the couch and appreciate her.

It is invariably in those moments when she is at her craziest that I am most aware of my love for her. That isn't a coincidence. Her craziness serves as a reminder that *all* women are crazy; the key is to find one whose craziness suits you.

When I think of the collection of neuroses and disorders I dated when I was single, I feel blessed to have found a woman whose greatest quirk is her ability to max out a credit card. I have married friends who occasionally wax nostalgic for their single days—mostly I think they have just run out of conversation. Either that or they are congenitally insane. People who reminisce fondly about dating are blocking out all the disasters and focusing only on the few great nights, like the time they got lucky with the stewardess, or that college dorm where they had two girls at the same time. Those are isolated, fleeting moments in a sea of otherwise torturous experience. If that is all you choose to remember, fine. But be aware that *no* experience is without good moments. (I'm sure that even during the sacking of Rome there were a few decent nights; maybe they put on a play.)

Personally, I am incapable of reminiscing about my dating life without becoming physically sick, maybe in part because my first date ended with me retching on the floor of my parents' bedroom.

I was sixteen and I had a date with Synthia. (Even the name is sexy and, believe me, she was.) She was the most popular girl in school, and—for reasons known only to her—she decided she liked me.

We made plans to meet at a bar on a Friday night, so I called my buddy Chuck who was older and more experienced (not a virgin) and asked him one simple question.

"WhatthehelldoIdo?"

He gave me a simple reply. "Get her drunk."

So I did. Or, I tried.

I pulled out my fake ID and ordered a large carafe of white wine and somehow decided that if we got through the entire thing she would be drunk, even if it was I who was doing all the drinking. It wasn't long before I fell off the chair. Then she had to help me into a cab and escort me to my parents' apartment, where I vomited on the bedroom rug.

Sadly, that would prove to be among the best nights of my dating life.

Then, in college, I had my first experience with pregnancy. It happened the day I got stood up for lunch. I was supposed to meet my girlfriend in a diner at noon, but by twenty past my eggs were cold. I went back to my apartment to find Shelley on the couch, her face pink and puffy, her eyes swollen from crying.

"What's going on?" I asked.

She sniffled a little but did not actually speak, just rose and walked slowly to the bathroom. When she emerged she was carrying a small white stick, like a cotton swab, with a powder-blue tip. She held the stick in front of my eyes, like a lawyer presenting a murder weapon as evidence to a jury.

"What?" I asked.

"Look," she said. Her voice was raspy from crying.

"What is it?"

She sighed heavily. "You mean to tell me that you have no idea what this is?"

"Right."

"Not an inkling?"

"This could go on all day," I said. "What the hell is it?"

"I swear to God, men are just pathetic," she said, thrusting the stick within an inch of my nose. "This is a home pregnancy test. The fact that you are twenty-one years old and do not already know that is a conversation we shall save for another day. The topic I'd like to stick with right now is the fact that I have managed to turn this stick blue. I'll give you one guess what that means."

By then I had figured it out.

"Congratulations," she said.

It later turned out that a urinary tract infection had caused a false positive. She was not pregnant. She was also obviously not sane, because she wasn't *my* girlfriend. It wasn't even *her* I was supposed to meet for lunch. (That was another woman, who turned out to have been stuck in an elevator.) In her hysteria, Shelley forgot whom she was dating; it was my roommate who would have been on the hook if she had been knocked up. I never brought that part up to her when it was all over.

(By the way, the girl I was dating at the time wound up marrying a guy she met in the stuck elevator. He's a successful orthodontist, and I'm told they have three kids and live in Scarsdale.)

Fast-forward a few years: I was twenty-six and had a blind date with a woman who had just undergone breast-reduction surgery. She told me about it within five minutes. Was it *so* inappropriate for me to ask to see the results? Was it not clear I was kidding?

Apparently not to her.

Here was a woman with the courage to have surgery on her breasts but no sense of humor about it. She spent the entire first course lecturing me about the seriousness of the operation. She was in tears throughout the entrée. Coffee was out of the question; I was on my way home ten minutes after I finished my chicken piccata.

We actually went out a few more times, calling it quits only when she was transferred to Rio de Janeiro. The last thing I said to her was that I had been to Brazil in my youth and my most vivid recollection was of the topless sunbathing. I suggested she consider having her breasts reenlarged in order to make a more memorable impression. She didn't find that funny. I should have known.

Then there was the gal I affectionately remember as "Kabuki woman."

I don't recall her actual name, but I'll never forget the summer afternoon we spent by the pool at my health club. Fully aware of that plan, she nevertheless arrived wearing more makeup than Dustin Hoffman in *Tootsie*. Within fifteen minutes, the dripping began. By lunch, she was a Picasso painting. I'm not sure her nose was in the right place. Still, she showed no sign of self-consciousness, refusing even to wipe her face with a towel. (Had she actually dived into the water, I believe she'd have left an oil slick.)

So that didn't work out. Then, a few months later, I met a pretty emergency room doctor who worked eighty-hour weeks. As you might imagine, she had plenty of good stories, so the small talk was a rousing success. I remember thinking I really liked her, enough to wonder whether if I told my grandmother I was marrying a doctor it would make up for the fact that I wasn't one.

Then dessert came.

"You know, I must feel awfully comfortable with you," she said. "Normally I have a very difficult time eating in front of people."

I didn't say anything.

"I guess it's been this way since I was about sixteen," she continued. "I just can't eat in front of anyone. Even family isn't always easy."

"Is it a table-manners issue?"

Sometimes, the question that jumps to mind is best left unasked.

"I appreciate you trying to defuse this with humor," she said, "but honestly I'm not uncomfortable. That's what I mean—I feel I could eat anything in front of you."

"Why can't you eat in front of people?" I asked.

"When I was in college I was bulimic, which I got over my first year at med school, when I just pretty much stopped eating. After I collapsed the third time, I was diagnosed as clinically malnourished. Do you have any idea how rare that is among Americans who live above the poverty line?"

"Not really."

"I finally found a nutritionist I felt comfortable with, and she created a diet for me that would keep me healthy and not make me feel bloated. The problems are obvious—a lot of gas, for example—but you get used to that."

I quickly went over her dinner in my mind. A house salad and the Niçoise; that's a little tuna and a lot of roughage.

"Check, please," I said, aloud.

The restaurant where we had eaten was near enough to her apartment that we walked home, and while I found her company pleasant I could not shake the image of her vomiting and farting at the same time. Then we arrived at the building and a man came charging out from the lobby.

"Laura, you fucking bitch, what are you doing with this motherfucker?"

Those may not have been his exact words. It was something with a lot of *bitch*es and *motherfucker*s in it.

"I thought your name was Allison," I said.

"It was," she replied.

Those were the last words she ever spoke to me.

The point of all this is that most people are either disgusting or insane, and many of them are both. If you are fortunate enough to find someone who does not make you nervous and does not make you sick, grab her and hold on tight. In my particular case, I found a woman who eats and has her original breasts. I can't imagine needing more.

●　　●　　●

I went to see Dr. Gray this morning. It was a productive session but, as usual, I have some complaints. The biggest is that she has a remarkable knack for taking the obvious and making it sound profound.

Here's an example: I told her I am feeling guilty about my lack of excitement over the baby coming. My feelings, in fact, are so far from what I believe they should be that it frightens me. I told her that I often feel guilty over the way I react to situations that should cause me great joy.

So here's what she said: "Michael, you are predisposed to feeling guilty."

Then she nodded. So I nodded, and it was as though we had made some terrific breakthrough. It was not until I was in the cab that I realized she and I had both said the exact same thing.

It makes me wonder if this isn't just a waste of time. It seems to me that all she really does is get me to tell her things I already know; then she tells them back to me in a fancier way and we both act as though we're getting somewhere. But where the hell are we getting if all we've learned is something I already knew? Maybe *she's* getting somewhere; all I'm doing is running in circles.

So what am I paying her for?

Maybe it's the nodding. Maybe all I really need is more nodding.

For what it's worth, I would say that today I am feeling a tad overwhelmed by the enormity of it all. I don't feel full of joy or bliss or delight or ecstasy, just a bit in awe, the way I sometimes feel listening to Mozart or Elvis Costello, or reading John Irving, or seeing Picasso's *Guernica* or a really good Woody Allen movie. I am aware that everything in my life is about to change, and I am fighting my inclination to assume that change is always for the worse.

I guess on some level I just cannot believe that "someday" is now here. I don't quite know what to make of that. Someday used to be a fluid, nebulous eventuality—a time so far in the future it would surely never arrive. Now that it's here I feel like it should have come with a little more fanfare. Actually, it's a bit disappointing. I guess someday loses a lot of its allure when it comes with a date attached.

The Third Trimester: **Total Disarray**

WHAT A COLOSSAL blunder this was.

We were having dinner with my brother and sister-in-law on

Thursday, and they were bemoaning how they never get away since my nephew was born. I don't know if I was acting in the spirit of kinship or the spirit of Grey Goose vodka, but suddenly I heard myself saying, "Why don't you leave Edgar with us and go away for the weekend?"

Not since a ball rolled between the legs of Boston's Bill Buckner in the World Series has anyone committed an error of this magnitude.

The next day they're at a bed-and-breakfast in Vermont eating freshly baked muffins and I'm a hostage in my own home.

Edgar is almost three and named for his maternal grandfather, whom neither he nor I was ever privileged to meet. He may well be the only American boy named Edgar in the last forty years, but generally he is a likable child, though he does have two qualities I find challenging.

The first is that his nose is a faucet. Every year from October through March, the child's nose is in a perpetual state of running. His mother blames the problem on nursery school, telling me that once any child in the class gets a cold they all get it and the cycle does not end until spring. Well, color me skeptical but I am certain I have seen toddlers in the winter months who were not dripping. Every time the child gives me a hug I am down another sweater. By the time we got through this weekend I had thrown away a Prada turtleneck and was using a John Varvatos scarf as a handkerchief.

Note to self: Make a trip to the Gap before baby is born.

The other problem I have with Edgar is his endless supply of energy. From the instant the child awakens until he is forcibly banished to his crib, he never stops. He runs, jumps, screams, cries, throws balls, kicks cats, chases dogs, rolls in mud, stomps in puddles, buries himself in snowdrifts, covers himself with ice cream, crashes toy cars, jumps off walls, hides and seeks—and throughout the process never ceases asking questions. The first five minutes are exhilarating. The next fifteen are a struggle. By the hour it is exhausting, and anything beyond that is pure torture. I believe if they sentenced felons to fly coach to Hawaii with my nephew, the chance of repeat offenses would be cut in half before they got to L.A.

Another thing I learned this weekend is that the boy is not *really* toilet trained. What I mean by that is that during his waking hours he is capable of using the bathroom but at night he sleeps with a diaper, and—at least for this weekend—the movement of his bowels was exclusively a nocturnal activity.

How can I begin to describe the odor with which I was greeted upon opening the door to my guest room Saturday morning? I'm surprised it didn't singe off my eyebrows. All I could think to do was cover my nose and mouth, which I did with a thick necktie. Then I grabbed a garbage bag from the kitchen and stood the child in it while I peeled away his diaper. What remained attached to his body resembled a thick mousse. I lifted him beneath the arms and carried him to the dresser, upon which I draped a bedsheet I had resigned myself to discarding. Holding the child down with one hand, I ripped desperately at the package of baby wipes. By now I was sweating and Edgar was kicking and I realized with horror that his foot had found the growing pile of wipes and his heel was coated. When I felt the foot scrape against my shirt I abandoned the cause. I scooped the child up again and ran to the shower. It was the first time in my life that I entered a shower with clothing on, but I wasn't able to get undressed without putting the child down, and I *certainly* wasn't going to do that. So there we were in the shower, together, me in my clothes, holding the child upside down by the feet, allowing water to spray into the area between his legs while he sang, "It's raining, it's pouring."

Lunch was macaroni and cheese, which Edgar insisted upon eating with his own utensils. Suffice it to say that by the end of the meal he was wearing most of the cheese. That didn't especially bother me. After handling a substance that would have frightened away people who transport hazmats, washing the cheese off his skull seemed comparatively benign. Also, the cheese was so thick it seemed it would have to be binding, and if this child was planning on moving his bowels again I wanted a brick to come out.

No such luck.

I have no idea about the gastrointestinal workings of your average three-year-old, but somehow Edgar's insatiable metabolism managed to churn a heavy cheese sauce into the Sloppy Joe I found in his diaper when he awoke on Sunday. When that smell greeted me again, all I could think to do was go to the kitchen and pour a glass of Johnnie Walker Blue.

Then I found myself in an argument with my wife over whether or not Edgar should be allowed to watch the football game with me.

"I thought spending time with Uncle Mike was the whole point of this exercise," I argued, "and that is how I plan to be spending my time."

"But his mother said he is only allowed one hour of television per day."

"That doesn't apply to sports," I said.

"Why wouldn't it apply to sports?"

"Two reasons," I said. "The first is that you cannot watch one hour of a football game. It's ridiculous. Second, watching sports is not like watching regular TV."

"How is it not like watching regular TV?" she asked. "You're going to sit on the couch and watch, just like you would if it was *Sesame Street*."

There was no way to win this argument. There is no way to explain how watching sports is different from watching regular TV. You either get it or you don't. She didn't. Edgar and I watched the first quarter of the football game and that was it.

When my brother finally showed up at five o'clock I told him what a wonderful joy the weekend had been. Then I turned to my wife and told her I could not wait to get to work so I could relax. If this is what being a parent is going to be like, I'm never going to make it.

•   •   •

Reading that last paragraph over again, after having lived through the events of last night, I believe I may need to amend it. A week after writing the above, I have now come to the conclusion that there is no way the experience of being a parent can possibly be more trying than the pregnancy itself. Because, as tough as Edgar was, there was something disposable about him. Perhaps it is as simple as saying: He's a handful, but in a dispute between the two of us, I win. With my wife, that's not the case. I've never won a dispute with her in my life, including when she *wasn't* pregnant. And right now, I would put my money on her in a dispute with Lennox Lewis.

I suppose I am going to have to describe what happened last night. But be forewarned: It is not for the weak of heart. If you have a pacemaker, put this book down right now. We're going backward in time twelve hours, to a moment of clarity when the belief husbands have had since the beginning of time was proven beyond the shadow of a doubt.

Pregnancy sucks.

It does, mostly because there is no way to defeat it. Nothing I do— no amount of effort—is ever appreciated. Plus, anything I *don't* do is construed as a total lack of understanding and compassion for how hard this is for her. And any energy I spend on anything else is interpreted as insensitivity.

Compounding all this is that mine is a wife with an extremely low tolerance for discomfort, and right now she is highly uncomfortable. Supremely uncomfortable. Biblically uncomfortable. For starters: She is constantly hot, which is jarring because this is a woman who is normally *always* cold. She brought sweaters to Maui. But now she is roasting, which has thrown my equilibrium off completely. Just when I was growing accustomed to sleeping with the heat on in July, I find myself at Home Depot on consecutive Saturdays buying industrial-strength fans.

Then, right around the time I got used to her change in body temperature, the diarrhea began. This is just brutal. There is nothing my wife can eat that does not go through her before I have finished chewing. And this woman does not have a cast-iron stomach, even during the best of times. (Case in point: Our honeymoon, and me trying desperately to explain to the customs agents in Casablanca why we were traveling with tuna fish and Pop-Tarts; you haven't lived until you've been interrogated by five men who speak nothing but Arabic.)

At any rate, now whenever my wife is not sweating or racing to the bathroom she is busy yelling at me. It hardly matters what I have done. In fact, she yells more often about things I have *not* done. The volume of the yelling varies, depending on her level of discomfort, but the final sentence is always the same.

You just don't understand what I'm going through.

That is the seminal sentence of pregnancy. Since the beginning of time, men have not been able to understand what their wives are going through. Worse yet, we don't even have a parallel experience. All we can do is comfort the best we can, and duck when there is no other recourse. And no matter what happens, *never* joke about it.

I found that out the hard way last night.

It was a dinner party for five couples, and you need to understand that at these functions there is always a great deal of pressure on me to know everything there is to know about sports, and to be funny. And those just aren't always easy things to accomplish at the same time. So we're sitting with these doctor friends, having dinner, and everyone is bouncing sports questions off me, and then one of the doctors starts telling me that watching his kid play competitive basketball is the hardest thing he's ever had to do. He said he becomes so nervous he often cannot remain in the arena. In response, I told a story of how Phil Jackson once told me he was infinitely more nervous as a coach than he ever was as a player because he had no control over the action. (Phil never actually said that, but it made a great story.) The table was riveted; I had fulfilled the first part of my obligation. Now it was time to be funny.

"You know," I said, "it's sort of like being an expectant father. You just feel helpless. Sometimes I think pregnancy is actually harder on the husband."

Do you remember the commercials when E. F. Hutton would talk? That is how silent the room became. All the women leaned closer, as if they could not believe they had actually heard it. I glanced at the other men, hoping for support, but they bailed on me like Billy Zane fleeing the *Titanic*.

The looks on their faces said: "We love you, Greeny, but you're dead."

The drive home wasn't pretty. This is one I'm going to be hearing about for a while, like during her sixth trip to the bathroom last night, when she threw a dagger through the slightly ajar door.

"I guess this is actually harder on *you*," she shouted.

There is a lesson to be learned in this, one I will make sure to pass on to the unborn child. Especially if it is a boy. And it is very simple: All is fair in love, war, and comedy. But wherever you go and whatever you do, never kid around about labor pain in front of a bunch of mothers.

●　　●　　●

Just when I thought things couldn't possibly get worse, this morning I got a flat tire on my way to work. That couldn't have sucked more. It was four o'clock in the morning, I was stranded on the side of the highway, it was cold, and the underside of my front right tire looked like corned beef hash.

I know people who, in that situation, would leap from the car and do a quick change. I can't tell you how much I hate those people.

I am completely helpless when things break. I can't fix them and I don't even try to, because if I fixed something I would never be convinced it wasn't still broken. I would never ride in a car I had put the tires on myself, for example, for fear they would fly off at the exact moment I was passing a gasoline truck.

First thing, I called my roadside assistance company. A generic answering service took down my number and promised that someone would return the call within thirty minutes. She said that as though thirty minutes was a rapid turnaround time. I tend not to agree. I could call my congressman and someone would get back to me in less than thirty minutes. It seemed entirely too long to have to wait, but there was nothing I could do; I was trapped by my own helplessness.

My next call was to 911. I explained to the operator that I was on the side of the highway and it was urgent that someone help me because millions of people were counting on me.

"What do you mean millions of people?" she asked.

"I host a radio show," I said. "I have an audience of over three million people and if I can't make it to work, those people will have to suffer their morning commutes without the entertainment they have come to depend on."

"I've never heard of you," she said. "Where are these millions of people?"

"They are all over the country."

"Well, I don't know any of them."

"I don't want to get into demographics," I explained, "but it's a sports show, so the audience is specialized."

"I've heard of Howard Stern," she said. "Are you Howard Stern?"

Obviously, this was a slow night for emergencies.

"Listen," I said, "I have no reason to make any of this up. I really do have a lot of people counting on me and if they can't listen to the show, there could be an increase in the incidence of road rage. I have to believe that isn't in either of our best interests."

She thought about it for a minute. "All right, tell me where you are."

I described as best I could my location and thanked her profusely.

"An officer should be there within an hour," she said, and hung up.

An hour.

One by one, cars whizzed past, none even slowing at the sight of me, which was just fine. The only thing worse than being stuck alone at four in the morning would be being stuck with whoever might think to stop and say hello.

With nowhere left to turn, I popped the trunk and began to root around until I found the tire-changing kit that came with the car; it was startlingly small. My golf clubs were in the way, so I pulled them out and stood them on the ground. The head of the driver cast an eerie shadow in the moonlight.

Then I dialed in to the studio to talk to my producer, who is a handy bastard and could probably change this tire in less time than it would take me to repack the trunk.

"I'm thirty miles away and I have a flat," I said. "I'm back here with the tools."

"Congratulations on getting the trunk open."

"Up yours," I said. "You're going to have to talk me through this."

"There is no way you're going to be able to do this," he said. "Have you called Triple-A?"

"It's going to take forever. My only chance of getting there in time is if you and I do this right now."

"Fine," he said. "Tell me this: Which one of the tools you are looking at right now is the jack?"

I stared at the mess of metal instruments. "I'll call you when the cops get here," I said.

Long before the roadside assistance called me back I saw the police car approaching. (It is a curious moment to feel elation at the sight of a squad car, but just then it was like being stranded on a desert island and seeing the distant lights of an approaching cruise ship.)

"Gentlemen, I can't tell you how much I appreciate this," I said.

"Let's see what we have here," one of the cops said.

He climbed from his car and walked over to the side of mine, shining a flashlight that was connected to his jacket. The other officer never looked up from his seat. He appeared to be eating a sandwich.

"Hey, mister!" It was the cop by my car, shouting to me. "This might take a little time."

With nothing else to do, I pulled the pitching wedge out of my golf bag and took a few practice swings. Then I looked back into the squad car. The second cop still hadn't looked up. He was definitely eating a sandwich.

Then the first cop shouted again. "I'm not sure I can help you with this."

Oh no.

"A lot of these foreign cars require an air jack, and we aren't equipped with those," he said.

This was a catastrophe. I looked pleadingly into the squad car, hoping for a miracle, but the second officer still didn't look up from his sandwich.

"You can't leave me," I said. "You have to do something."

"Sir, there isn't anything I *can* do."

"Listen," I begged, "if you leave me here, and then you come back tomorrow, I'm still going to be here. So at least ask your partner to leave me the sandwich so I don't starve to death."

The officer burst out laughing. "Listen, buddy," he said, "maybe I can give you a ride up to where you're going."

"That sounds great," I said. "What will we do with my car?"

"That's up to you."

I leaned forward in a conspiratorial whisper. "Maybe we can leave your partner here until the roadside assistance shows up. He doesn't seem particularly focused."

I didn't get a chance to find out how the cop would have reacted to that because before he could say a word, bright lights flashed upon us and a tow truck pulled up behind the squad car.

"Someone here call for a tire change?"

The miracle had happened. It came in the form of a guy with an air jack. It took him two minutes to replace my tire, and then he was off without a word.

"How did that happen?" I asked.

"My partner radioed for help while I was taking a look at the situation," the cop said. "I think it was while you were practicing your golf swing."

I looked into the car. The second officer was still eating his sandwich.

"What do I owe you guys?" I asked.

"You owe us a decent show starting in less than an hour," he said. "You'd better haul your ass up there. And when you talk about my Red Sox, say nice things."

As I pulled away and the bright light from the squad car dimmed in my rearview mirror, I thought to myself what a strange job mine was. Just the other night, at the dinner party, being a little famous had screwed me. This morning it had saved me, in the most unexpected place and time. There is nowhere on earth you feel less like a celebrity than the side of a highway in the dark of night. I wonder if the cop knew who I was all along, and if he would have done the same for anyone. I wonder, too, if the second cop really *had* radioed for help, or if that was just my own roadside assistance I had called for earlier. Plus, I find myself wondering what kind of sandwich it was. What a nuisance, to begin my day with so many unanswered questions.

·   ·   ·

We have now entered a highly dicey area. The arrival of this child is bearing down on us like a locomotive and we still don't have any idea what we are going to name it. It seems to me that this is the most important decision we're ever going to make. That puts a lot of pressure on us and, frankly, we're not dealing with it well.

Well, mostly my wife isn't.

This is really getting to her, which means it is getting to me too, by osmosis. And there doesn't appear to be any end in sight, despite an ingenious plan I *thought* would put me out of this misery.

I have several friends who have made deals—essentially business transactions—with their wives when it came to naming children. One guy got a new set of golf clubs in exchange for naming his son Zachary. Another bought his wife a diamond brooch so he could name his daughter Emmanuelle. I must confess, the monetary element of those arrangements left me cold. But I liked the idea of presenting some sort of deal, so I made the following suggestion: She would write down her top five choices and I would do the same; then we would flip a coin. The loser of the toss would have to choose a name from the list of the winner. I thought it was ingenious, and—much to my shock—she agreed. I thought I was home free. All we needed was the names, so we further agreed to a forty-eight-hour research period.

I spent the next day in the library, where I discovered it would be easy to have a nervous breakdown making this decision. It was difficult just narrowing down the reference books. There were more than a dozen on baby names alone. I chose *The Complete Dictionary of English First Names*, which presented more than eleven thousand options, and started at the beginning.

Alphabetically, the first name in the English language is Aaron.

"In the Bible, Aaron is the older brother of Moses. The name originates from the Hebrew, and means 'shining' or 'mountain.' "

That confused me immediately. I don't speak Hebrew, but how could a word possibly mean both "shining" and "mountain"? What if one is trying to describe a shining mountain? Would it be an Aaron Aaron? I couldn't see myself choosing such an indecisive name.

I flipped to the feminine names, where the first entry was Abbe. I have always liked that name, though that isn't how I thought it was spelled. What I discovered is that it can be spelled any of four ways, all of which are short forms of Abigail, which itself is a variant form of the Hebrew Avigayil, which means "a father's joy."

Bingo, I had my first name.

In the interest of not boring you with the entire alphabet, here are the names I eventually chose.

Boys: Jared, Jonathan, William.

Girls: Abby, Veronica.

I awoke the following morning ready to go. Then I saw her list. There were ten names on it. That was two times too many.

"We agreed on five names," I said.

"Obviously, five boys and five girls," she said.

"But you didn't say that."

"That's what I meant."

Over the years, I have come to learn that "That's what I meant" is the most significant phrase in my wife's repertoire. She treats those four words as though they can explain away anything. Once she told me her mother wanted to come stay with us from Sunday until Tuesday. I said that was fine. It was not until her mother was comfortably unpacked in my guest room that I found out the Tuesday she was referring to was two weeks away.

"You didn't tell me she was staying two weeks," I said. "You just said she was staying until Tuesday."

"That's what I meant," she said.

Anyway, I wasn't going to make too much fuss over this discrepancy until I looked more closely at the list.

Boys: Eric, Walker, Harrison, Scottie.

Girls: Clair, Elizabeth, Kate, Lily, Jill, Claire.

She'd gone six and four. How could she have *meant* five of each if she'd listed six and four?

"I couldn't come up with any more boys' names I liked," she explained.

"And you listed the name Claire twice," I said.

"I did not."

I pointed to the list.

"They're spelled differently," she said. "The spelling completely changes the feel of the name."

I scratched my head. "So what you're saying is that even though they are pronounced exactly alike, you are counting them as two different names."

"That's correct."

There didn't seem much point in fighting over it, especially since I sort of liked Kate and I could have lived with Eric or Harrison. I was ready to play. I thought it a bad sign that she didn't even look at my list, but I took a quarter out of my pocket anyway.

"Wait a minute," she blurted just as I was about to toss it.

"What is it?"

"I'm nervous," she said.

"What are you nervous about?"

"I'm not sure I picked the right names," she said.

We both stood there silently until I realized I didn't know if she was waiting for me to toss the coin or I was waiting for her to tell me she was ready. There wasn't any way to find out without going for it, so I tossed the coin in the air.

"What are you doing?" she asked before it hit the ground.

"I didn't know what you wanted me to do," I said.

"But we didn't decide who is heads and who is tails."

Now she was giving me that look that says I might be the stupidest man on the face of the earth. I had a quick idea to save it, though. The coin had just skidded to a halt, so I stepped on it and left my foot over it.

"Which do you want?" I asked, proud of the save. "Heads or tails?"

"We can't count this toss," she said. "You saw which one it was."

"What difference does it make if I saw?" I asked. "You didn't see and you're the one picking heads or tails."

"No," she said, "it's not fair if you know which one it is."

I didn't feel like turning this into an argument so I merely bent and picked up the coin.

"Which was it?" she asked.

"What?"

"Was it heads or tails?"

"What difference does *that* make?"

"I just want to know," she said. "Can't I just know?"

It was heads, I told her. Then I held out the coin in an open palm. "Now this is it," I said. "Do you want heads or tails?"

"I'll take heads," she said.

I tossed the coin into the air. It came down between us and clanged loudly on the hardwood floor. Then, just as it came to rest, she stepped on it.

"I think I want to change my choice," she said.

"You mean the names?"

"No," she said. "I think I may want tails."

This had already taken most of the morning. "Take your time," I said. "If you want to switch to tails, that's fine with me."

"Because you think it's heads, don't you?"

"I have no way of knowing which it is. It's a fifty-fifty shot. Choose whichever one you want."

Ten minutes later she chose tails. It was heads. I had won. I pointed to my list, still folded in her hand.

"There you go, honey," I said, sweet as I could. "I hope you like one of these names."

She didn't even look. "No," she said, "I can't do this."

"You don't even know what they are," I said. "For all you know, Claire is on the list."

"I don't even like Claire anymore."

"Not with either spelling?" I asked.

"That's correct."

"Well, honey," I said, "we agreed to this deal, so you *have* to pick one of my names."

"I changed my mind," she said, and left the room.

As sentences go, "I changed my mind" is a lot like "That's what I meant."

Ultimately, she didn't come out of the bedroom for so long that I decided to go to the gym. That was Sunday. It is now Wednesday and we are no closer to choosing a name. But I'll tell you this: If I were a betting man, I'd put my money on Claire. Or Clair.

●   ●   ●

Last night, my unborn child saved my life.

It happened in the middle of a business trip to Washington, during the worst night I've ever had. It happened after all the business was done, meetings attended, hands shaken; then, at dinner, I made the irrevocable error of ordering tuna tartare on a Sunday night. How a street-smart kid like me could do something so stupid I cannot say. Somehow I'd managed to live all these years without anyone warning me not to order raw fish on Sunday. (It seems the chances of disaster increase exponentially after Friday. Last night those chances caught up with me.)

I was alone in my room at the St. Regis Hotel, sleeping peacefully, when I was awakened by a distant rumbling in my intestine. At first I had no idea the trouble I was in; I just called the butler and asked for ginger ale and Pepto-Bismol. It was not until an hour later, when I was curled up like a shrimp, that I knew this was an issue beyond the pink stuff.

The butler was a Middle Eastern woman about my age, wearing a tuxedo. "What can I get for you, sir?" she asked.

"I don't know," I said. "My stomach is a mess. What have you got?"

"Perhaps something cold," she said, with what sounded like a British accent. "Perhaps some ice cream."

The first thing that occurred to me was how different those words sound when you place the emphasis on the second (the *cream* rather than the *ice*). Then it hit me that she was obviously a complete idiot. I'm no doctor, but I know better than to offer ice cream to someone who is nauseous.

"God, no," I said, "I think I need a doctor."

"We have one on call," she said.

"Good," I said, sliding out of bed and crawling to the bathroom. "I'll be out soon."

After what may have amounted to the worst ten minutes of my life, when everything I had eaten since the seventh grade had vacated the premises, I stumbled back into the bedroom. The butler was on the sofa, tuxedo slightly askew.

"Are you all better, sir?" she asked.

I was doubled over at the waist, wearing nothing but a pair of boxer shorts, holding my head to keep it from dragging on the floor. How awful could I have looked when I got here that my current appearance might constitute "all better"?

"Is the doctor almost here?" I asked.

"Would you like me to call him, sir?"

I fell to my knees. "You haven't called him yet?"

"I wasn't certain that was your wish," she said.

Now I hated her. I told her to call the doctor, and I think I used the word *fuck* several times. Then I went back into the bathroom, where my unborn child saved my life.

As I lay on the cold tile with my cheek on the bath mat, dry heaving with absolutely nothing left inside me, I looked up and saw a window. I decided to jump out. It was *that* bad; no matter how frightening the fall might be, and how painful the collision, at least it would be over quickly. The idea of staying on the floor in full-fledged gastro-intestinal spasm was too horrendous to consider. I decided to try to size up the window. I struggled to my feet, pulling myself up with the shower curtain, and made my way over. But before I got there I came across a shelf with a dazzling array of accoutrements, and even in my state I could not pass those without a glance. There was lotion, face cream, hair tonic, aftershave, deodorant, a shaving brush, and three different kinds of soap: one for face, another for shower, and the third for sensitive skin.

"Gentle enough," it said, "for a baby to use."

I read that label over again, three or four times, and just like that I knew I wasn't jumping out any window. No matter how horrendous the food poisoning, I couldn't leave a baby without a dad.

After an eternity, the door opened and in came two paramedics, who scooped me off the floor and placed me in a wheelchair. From behind, I heard the butler call.

"Is there anything else I can do, sir?"

"Bring my clothes!"

So off we went, the emergency medical technicians, my butler, and me, into an ambulance and off to the hospital. On the way I asked if anyone knew what time it was. The butler did: four in the morning. Between dry heaves, I also heard her offer a piece of gum to a paramedic, who declined. Then she offered a piece to me. What an idiot.

"Just don't get puke on my Prada shoes," I said.

At the hospital, they transferred me onto a gurney and left me in the emergency room, alone with the butler.

"Where shall I lay your clothes, sir?" she asked.

"Just get a doctor."

Eventually someone in blue scrubs emerged from behind a curtain and introduced himself. I didn't catch the name and I didn't care; I just wanted drugs.

"What can you give me, Doc?" I begged. "If you can knock me out for a while, that would be best."

"Oh, I'm not the doctor," the man said. "I'm from the administrative office. I need to collect your insurance information."

"Oh my God," I said, and rolled onto my side in dry heaves.

"I'll just need your card," the man said.

"I'm in my underwear," I said. "Where the hell do you think I'm carrying my insurance card?"

"Perhaps it is in one of your pockets, sir," the butler said, rifling through the pockets of my pants and jacket. "No, sir," she finally said. "There's nothing."

I looked up to see the guy in scrubs scratching his head with a pencil. He was heavyset and balding and, suddenly, I hated him even more than I hated the butler.

"Sir," he asked, "do you by any chance know your insurance policy number?"

I closed my eyes. "Please, just get me a doctor."

"Sir, I'm afraid I need some proof of insurance."

"Listen," I said, managing to sit up a little, "do you see this woman in a tuxedo carrying my clothes for me at four o'clock in the morning? She is my butler from the St. Regis Hotel! Are we really concerned that I don't have health insurance?"

It was a dickish thing to say, I know, but the doctor came pretty quickly after that. I don't remember much of what happened next—they put a tube in my arm and soon the nausea subsided. I think I fell asleep for a while, then left the hospital at around noon. I never did see the butler again. She left my clothes neatly folded on a chair by my gurney; I don't even recall her telling me she was going to go.

When I checked out I left a note of thanks at the hotel, with special praise for her. I hope she saw it. Looking back, I think she did everything she could have and maybe more. If she is a complete moron, well, that isn't really her fault, and to hold it against her would be unfair. I doubt situations like mine are covered in the butler's handbook, anyway.

Note to unborn child: I owe you one.

*   *   *

I suppose it could be taken as a discouraging sign of things to come that the due date is now less than two weeks away and I still haven't written that letter. In fact, as I sit down now to try, all I know for sure is that I am less certain than ever of how to do it.

By that, I mean: I want to write it, I just don't know *what* I want to write.

I suppose part of it should be about sports. Because, for me, everything is a little about sports. Actually, this could be a great opportunity to explain just how beautiful sports can be, especially in a world where that is becoming increasingly difficult to see.

But the letter cannot be *just* about sports. It should really be about heroes. That's what I loved about sports when I was a kid; I loved the guys who played them. I had real heroes, close enough for me to reach out and touch but still far enough away that they remained perfect. That's the whole key to being a hero. Heroes don't have flaws, at least none you can see. The trouble today is that athletes are too close, too accessible, their warts too visibly on display. We know so much about them it's hard to look past all the paternity suits and unregistered handguns. It was so much better before we knew about that stuff. Maybe ignorance really is bliss. But I don't think I want to write that in a letter to an unborn child.

So what *do* I want to write?

Maybe I'll write about my first experiences covering sports, and all the heroes who disappointed me. Which reminds me of a line from a movie I love, called *My Favorite Year*. In the movie there is an impressionable young writer who is assigned to look after a fading movie star, and the writer wants desperately to believe that what he has seen on the screen—which has meant so much to him—is real.

"Don't tell me this is you life size," he says. "I can't use you life size. I need my Alan Swanns as big as I can get them."

As a kid, I loved Joe Namath and O. J. Simpson, and Mickey Mantle, and the announcer Marv Albert. Those were my Alan Swanns. They were all pretty big. And it's been painful watching them shrink as I've grown up.

It was torturous watching Mickey disintegrate before our eyes; he lived as a hero, but he died as a cautionary tale.

The humiliation of Marv Albert was among the most unsightly and stunning news stories of my lifetime.

The sentence "O. J. Simpson is armed and dangerous" is still the most shocking phrase I have ever heard uttered on television.

And then there is Broadway Joe. My idol, the biggest Alan Swann I ever had. Until one night he was so drunk on national television that he asked one of my colleagues if he could kiss her. I had to turn the television off.

None of those—with the exception of O.J.—changed the fact that I admire these men greatly, as I always will. But they were diminished, each in his own way, which is probably more my fault than theirs. Maybe no one's reality could ever live up to the imagination of his fans. Maybe the bigger your Alan Swanns are, the more certain they are to fall. But that doesn't make it easier to watch.

I'll tell you one who never fell, though, at least not for me.

Michael Jordan.

The first time I met him was in January 1991, five months before he won his first championship. The Bulls had played the Nets that night, and afterward I stood in line with twenty other reporters outside the locker room in the bowels of the old Chicago Stadium. When we were herded in, I was amazed at how cramped the space was; the locker rooms at my high school were bigger. I was crammed between two camera guys and didn't know the protocol, but at that moment I didn't care because I was too distracted by the sight of Scottie Pippen naked. I tried to look away, but everywhere I turned there was a famous player nude: Horace Grant, John Paxson, B. J. Armstrong. I remember wondering if I was the only one who realized how ridiculous it looked.

Then Michael walked in.

He was dressed in suit pants and suspenders, a monogrammed shirt and silver tie. He was bigger than I'd expected, larger than life, more magnetic than any person I have ever seen. I listened to him in awe, forgetting to turn on my tape recorder. (That's how I managed not to get paid for the first game I ever covered.)

But that was the first day of my career watching Michael Jordan, and it was more than a job; it was a privilege. And an education. Because Jordan was not only the greatest player in the history of sports, he was also an inspiration to anyone who *really* paid attention to what made him great.

It was all in his head. It was all in his confidence and competitiveness and determination and mental toughness. I traveled with Michael Jordan for years and never once saw him waver. I never saw him afraid. Michael Jordan was the most supremely self-confident human being that ever lived. His unshakable faith in his ability is what set him apart, made him special. It is what enabled him to fly.

My most vivid memory of Jordan, the one I will see behind closed eyes forever, came when he was playing baseball. I was there, in Sarasota, Florida. I saw every game he played, which means I saw the first hit he ever got. It had taken an embarrassingly long time and then it came not with a roar but a squeak; he beat out a dribbler up the third-base line. There couldn't have been more than a thousand people in the stands that rainy night, and there weren't more than a handful of reporters to see it. I was one of them. Afterward, I went to the clubhouse and watched Jordan's teammates give him a beer shower in front of his locker. Then he answered a few questions. Then all the reporters were herded off to file our stories. But something moved me to look back, to glance at Jordan one more time. And that is the image of him I will always have. Sitting in front of his locker in an empty room, nude except for a towel around his waist, dripping in sweat and cheap beer, with the widest smile I ever saw on his face.

This is a man I watched climb mountains and bathe in adoration most people could never imagine, but I never saw him more proud of himself than he was that night. There is a lesson in that, I think. Something about celebrating the dribblers, no matter how meaningless they may seem.

But I don't think any of this is getting me closer to a letter to the unborn child. I certainly can't write the whole thing about sports or about Michael Jordan; I would like the child to think I have *some* perspective, even if that isn't actually the case.

Maybe I'm just not ready to write any such letter, largely because I don't have anything important enough to say. It is painfully obvious that nothing I've ever done is worthy of wasting my unborn child's time. I guess I'll just skip the letter, or at least put it off until something profound occurs to me. The child is probably better off, anyway. For a man who makes his living with words, I'm often painfully inarticulate; it's just as well the kid doesn't find that out too soon. I wouldn't want to be a disappointment, not with something this important. Imagine, a grown man writing a majestic letter to an unborn child about sports; I'm embarrassed even to have considered it. I think I'll just keep notes along the way in hopes that eventually they will amount to a full-fledged letter.

Note to child: Wherever you may go, and whatever you may do, and however long you may live, my first wish for you as your father is that you always have your Alan Swanns as big as you can get them.

●　　●　　●

I went to the grocery store today. That, in itself, is worthy of mention because I almost never go to the grocery store. But it is also worthy of mention because I had an epiphany while I was there.

I should begin by admitting that I've been especially anxious these last few weeks. I find that whenever I look at people with small children they always look harried and frazzled and frustrated. None of them look quietly contented, which is the emotion I am really hoping fatherhood will bring me. I was just about ready to give up on that.

Then I went to the supermarket.

Normally, the housekeeper does the grocery shopping, but she's in Panama this week tending to a sick uncle or chickens or something, and my wife is—as her doctor described her—a "ticking time bomb," so I found myself stuck with this task I despise. There is almost nothing I do not prefer to shopping for groceries. I hate the configuration of the aisles, I hate the lack of natural light, and I especially hate the fat people buying food that will make them fatter. I also don't like the women in housedresses, reading about glamorous movie stars in magazines they put in the wrong slots when it's their turn to pay. And I don't like how quickly the woman checking my groceries runs items over the scanner; I have no control over the process. One of my items could easily come up as "Nazi Home Starter Kit, $14.95" and there'd be nothing I could do about it. Plus, I don't like the haphazard manner in which the kid bagging my groceries throws things around. I understand that his is not challenging work, but I see no reason why he must take out his frustration on my eggs. Really, could his pathetic flirtation with the heavily pierced bagger in the next aisle be so important it cannot wait three minutes?

I wish the supermarket were more like a department store, where salespeople depend on a commission. Would you buy clothes from the people who work in a supermarket? Me neither, yet we allow them to handle the food that goes into our bodies. Imagine a trained salesperson in the breakfast-cereal aisle, with a wealth of knowledge about the fat content in one brand and the supply of vitamins and minerals in another. Wouldn't you shop in that store?

At any rate, I was approaching the supermarket this morning with a sense of dread when I almost ran into an old friend. Literally. I almost ran her over in the parking lot. My attention was on parking spaces, so I was looking everywhere but directly in front of me, where a pretty woman was pushing a cart with a little boy seated inside. The child was too big to fit his legs through the slots so he was inside the actual cart, as though his mother had found him in the toddler aisle and was going to buy him. (And if she painted a bar code on the boy's thigh, I bet the checker would run him over the scanner without even noticing.) Anyway, as I waved and mouthed an apology, I was overcome by the notion that I had seen the woman before. She had already gone inside before it dawned on me that she was a woman I went to high school with, longer ago than I care to think about. She was among the prettiest girls in school and still was pretty, though in a less sexy way. I found that I remembered a lot more about her than I would have expected. I remembered the first names of both her parents, and the classes we were in together, and a night when I danced with her at a party and thought I might kiss her until she started making out with some guy in his thirties.

Then I was out of my car, walking through the parking lot, and I found myself wondering how she had managed to be here. I wanted to go in and find her, and ask about everything that had happened in her life since graduation. Not because I was so interested, but because I wanted to know how fate had managed to lead her to this spot at this time. In a world as large as ours, what is the likelihood that two people can go fourteen years without seeing each other and then suddenly wind up in the same supermarket at the same time? How did it happen? How had she decided to do her shopping today, at the same time I had?

Ultimately, I opted against tracking her down. I can't imagine she would want to recount the story of her life to a guy she danced with once in high school, particularly with frozen foods and her son thawing simultaneously in her cart. But as I approached the automatic doors, I found myself wondering something else.

How did *I* get here?

What had happened in my life that had led me to this spot, at this moment? I stopped dead in my tracks and looked all around me, pondering the endless series of decisions that had brought me to that exact moment in time. I enjoyed it. In fact, I recommend it. Stop sometime and ask yourself, How did I get here? How did life lead me to this place in time? You might find it therapeutic, particularly at the supermarket.

Once inside, shopping and being careful to avoid bumping into the woman, I found myself staring at a guy in the cheese department. He was a nicely dressed fellow, a few years older than me, pushing a cart overflowing with baby groceries (baby food, wipes, diapers) and beer. He was also whistling. Now, if there's one thing I cannot tolerate, it is a public whistler. No one alive has a whistle so melodic that others should have to hear it. So I gave him my best hard stare, the one that usually silences the public whistler, but it didn't work. The guy never glanced up. He just walked up and down the aisles, looking at everything and nothing at the same time, never breaking stride, never stopping the whistling. It seemed to me he didn't even realize he was whistling. He just looked happy to be out on a sunny morning, doing his shopping, with his family waiting at home. He had sort of a light, sunny, oblivious grin that became contagious as I watched him. Before I knew it, I was following him up and down the aisles.

Suddenly, and for the first time, public whistling didn't bother me. In fact, I walked away whistling myself. And it occurred to me, as I whistled up and down the aisles, that this is what life is all about. Life is not one long, continuous miracle. Life is a series of thousands of tiny miracles. It's not about the days when things happen you'll never forget, like the first time you see the *Mona Lisa* or when your boss gives you a raise. Life is much smaller than that. Life is about moments just like this. When you're whistling in the supermarket and you don't even know it.

SECOND TRIP
to the Supermarket

October 2001 – January 2002

Under Siege

I like to think of myself as a forgiving person.

I believe in giving people second chances. And third chances. And fourth, and fifth, and tenth chances. That applies to both my personal and my professional lives.

I appreciate the idea of forgiveness, probably because I screw things up all the time.

Like, once I threw a brand-new red towel into a washing machine filled only with whites. By the time they hit the dryer, they were pinks.

You live, you learn.

I remember when my wife and I were first dating, for Valentine's Day I got talked into buying her a gaudy, lacy, skin-tight nightgown from Victoria's Secret.

She married me anyway.

And she's put up with worse since. Like the time I tried to fix a lightbulb above the shower. (We had to move.) Or the time I left our passports in a hotel-room drawer in Greece. (We were detained.) Or the time I dragged her to see *Deuce Bigalow: Male Gigolo*. (We walked out.)

You forgive. It's what separates us from the animals.

And it applies in sports, too. Particularly with athletes who use drugs. I was in favor of giving Darryl Strawberry every chance they gave him, no matter how many times he got busted with cocaine and hookers. Likewise Steve Howe; anytime he was able to pry his face off the mirror, I was prepared to give him a ball and see if he could still throw it.

I believe in giving people every possible chance to redeem themselves.

But there is one exception. And that exception is steroids.

The guys who do steroids, I do not forgive. Them, I do not give a second chance. They are dead to me, and always will be, no matter how earnestly they might seek my compassion.

There is enormous speculation about just how widespread the use of steroids in sports is. In my opinion, it is worse than even the most cynical among us imagine. And that galls me to my core, because it is just so damned disrespectful.

This isn't about the message we send to kids. If we were really worried about the messages we send to kids, we would have to eliminate most of the movies, music, and television they see. I have to believe that steroids get lost amid all the gratuitous sex and hard-core violence our impressionable youth are exposed to.

No, this isn't about the kids. It's about us, the fans. After all, what are we but a bunch of wannabes? We're a bunch of guys who would desperately love to be ballplayers but can't.

Because we're not good enough.

I can live with that. So can you. We have to. Some guys are just luckier than us. Some guys are born bigger and stronger and faster, and they work and sacrifice and pay the price, and if they're really special they become the guys we pay to watch. And we envy them like crazy—oh, just once to know what it's like to hit a home run that wins a ball game! But that doesn't keep us from admiring them, because we know they earned it.

But what if they didn't?

What if the reason they're down there and we're up here

came from a syringe? What if the difference between them and us is grounds for a felony charge? What if it isn't real?

That we can't accept—I can't, anyway. That would destroy every bit of enjoyment I find in watching these games. That I cannot forgive.

Because regardless of how insignificant the act of hitting a baseball may actually be, to some of us it means everything. For some of us, sports are important well beyond rational perspective. I love sports and the men who play them. And I understand that—for those guys—baseball is a living. But they, in turn, must understand that for us it is a great deal more than that. And shame on them if they would devalue something so precious by cheating.

So to the ballplayers I say this: Don't tell me you love baseball if you would cheat at it. That is placing yourself ahead of the game, and no matter how much money you make, or how many home runs you hit, you are not more important than the game.

No one is.

Shame on you if you don't realize that.

•   •   •

Well, I guess I'm writing again.

I haven't opened this journal in nearly two years, haven't felt I needed to. I write only when I need to figure myself out, and for nearly two years, I think I've understood. But now I'm writing again, even though I'm not sure exactly why. I think it has something to do with crying and also with football, which is funny because no two things have less to do with each other.

The good news is that I have not been unhappy since the baby was born. Quite the opposite; I've been very happy. That's why I never wrote when she was a baby. (Which she isn't anymore; my little girl is almost two years old.) I didn't feel a need to write in this journal after she was born, not once, not even during those rough nights only new parents have, when it's two in the morning and you're in a rocking chair, trying to feed an infant who isn't hungry, trying to find anything on television, settling for reruns of *Rhoda*. I would say that was the low point of my daughter's first year: the night I was watching *Rhoda* at two in the morning and realized I had seen the same episode a few weeks before. So it was two in the morning and I was watching a rerun of a rerun of *Rhoda*, and my daughter was fast asleep in my arms with her teeth clenched against the nipple of a bottle, and I was afraid to move a muscle because if she woke up and started to cry again I was sure I'd take my own life.

But I never thought to write in this journal that night. Or the morning after. Or any morning after that, not in all this time. The transition went well. My wife was home the first few months, which helped a lot. My parents and in-laws helped as well. And we got a great deal of help from Lourdes. (I don't mean a blessing from the pope; Lourdes is our Panamanian nanny. She lives in.)

So everything was terrific.

Then last week, out of nowhere, I went off on that bizarre diatribe about steroids. That was totally unlike me; I have no idea where it came from. I've never much cared about steroids. Now, suddenly, I care? That seemed significant enough that I saved the transcript to show Dr. Gray, but that alone wouldn't have made me start writing again. What it *did* do was get me thinking. And the more I thought, the more I realized how emotional I've been about everything lately. I just can't stop crying, which is totally unlike me. I never cry. It isn't a macho thing; I just don't do it. But tonight I cried during a commercial for a soft drink. Then I yelled at a football coach. And immediately after that I opened to this page, and here we go. Pen in hand. Back and more confused than ever. (Wetter, too, from the crying.)

The crying is a new phenomenon. As I said before, it didn't start right after the baby was born. I know a lot of guys cry when their children are born but I did not; I was much too frazzled to cry. That was a long day, filled with sweating and pushing and shouting encouragement. There are two things I remember most about that day, the first being the sound of my father's voice. It was moments before the baby came, and my wife was panting and breathing and sweating, facing the door in the delivery room, while I stayed by her head and told her how great she was doing. (Of course I didn't really know if she was doing great; I had nothing to compare it to. But saying, "Honey, I think you could pick it up a little, I'm getting hungry!" seemed out of the question.)

Anyway, it was getting close—I could tell from the game-faces on the doctor and delivery nurse—when there was a momentary lull and I heard my father's voice. He and my mother had arrived to see their first grandchild, which was wonderful, but then a bloodcurdling fear shot up my spine. What if they went into the wrong room? What if the door to the delivery room opened just now and it was my parents, mistakenly thinking this was the waiting room? They would have been face-to-face with their grandchild—except the grandchild's face was still inside my wife.

What the hell would happen then? Certainly they could never see us again. My wife would never get over that; either we would have to move away or I would have to kill both my parents. There was no third option.

Mercifully, that didn't happen. As quickly as the voice appeared it was gone again; no doubt they had found the waiting room and now they were just waiting for the blessed news to come. That was quite a relief; it was also the first thing I'll always remember about that day.

Then there was another contraction and suddenly our room was once again filled with my wife's deafening cries and the beeping from all the machines and the encouragement from the doctor and the nurse. Meanwhile, I was so relieved that my parents had not just gone face-to-cervix with my wife that I think I overdid it. I began shouting encouragement again, too enthusiastically, and when that contraction faded my wife grabbed me by the arm and pulled my face to hers.

"Shut the fuck up, Michael," she hissed, in a voice I had never heard and hope never to hear again. "Shut the fuck up!"

Not that I blame her. I probably needed to shut the fuck up.

Anyway, that's the other thing I will always remember from the delivery room. That didn't make me cry, either. (It made me tremble a little, but not cry.) Nor did I cry when the baby came out, or when the doctor said, "It's a girl!," or when I kissed my wife on the forehead and told her how proud I was, or when I told my parents, or phoned family and friends, or even when they gave me the little pink bundle to hold for the first time.

I cried a week later, when I had to go on the road. When I saw the car pull into the driveway, I kissed my two girls good-bye. The bigger one kissed me back. The little one was fast asleep in her arms, as sweet as anything I've ever seen. As I left the house I couldn't hear a thing over the roar of the mowers my lawn service was using; they are three Spanish-speaking guys with industrial-strength riding mowers who knock off my property in about ten minutes. I had never noticed how loud they were until just then, when I was getting in the limo and trying to shout, "I love you!" to my wife and newborn baby watching me from the doorway, but I knew they couldn't hear me over the roar of the lawn mowers.

Then the driver was backing out of the driveway and I asked him to stop before we pulled away. I had the window open and I could see my wife was still in the doorway, holding the baby, watching us drive away, so I waved with everything I had, waved like I had never waved before.

That was when I started to laugh.

Because one of the Spanish-speaking guys, who was mowing the area between the car and the house, stopped and waved back at me. In fact, he never turned to see that it was actually my family I was waving to; he kept waving all the time as the driver pulled away. He obviously thought I was waving good-bye to *him*, and I assume he will always think so. I began to laugh, so hard I also started to cry, and then I called my wife from my cell phone and found she was laughing too, and crying at the same time, just like I was. It was a memorable way to begin my first business trip as a father.

As I recall, I realized, right there in that car, that it was the first time my daughter had made me cry. I remember I also thought it was certain not to be the last. But you never forget the first time.

Everything went pretty well after that until lately, when I've started crying again, only this time I'm crying over nothing. It's like my entire life is being spent in the audience of *Terms of Endearment*. (Or *Brian's Song*. That always gets me.) But it's one thing to get emotional at the movies; tonight I cried at a commercial with some little kid playing basketball with Michael Jordan. It made me think of that other commercial, years ago, when another kid gave "Mean" Joe Greene a Coke and Greene drank it and then tossed the kid his jersey, and the kid shouted, "Thanks, Mean Joe!" Do you remember that? It was the greatest commercial ever. But I probably shouldn't be crying over it thirty years later.

As I dabbed my eyes with a tissue, the football game I was watching came back on, and it was then that I lost my mind. I'm just lucky I didn't lose my job at the same time. It was among the strangest things to ever happen to me, especially when you consider how much I love football.

(To me, football is the greatest sport of all, the greatest game in the world, the true American pastime. I love the game and the men who play it. I love the fearlessness and the gore; I love the blood. I love the way the players look when they lose. I love the ones who wear short sleeves when it's twenty below. I love the look on the face of the referee when he makes a call the crowd doesn't like. I love the way Sunday feels when it's getting dark outside and the television is the only light in the house. I love the announcers who feel a need to explain that stopping the run is important. I love the music they play when they're going to scroll the scores across the bottom, and I love when they throw it to the studio so we can see Kansas City return a punt for a touchdown. I love everything about pro football, and my absolute favorites are the coaches.

There are no tougher, more powerful men in the world than football coaches. I think Mike Ditka could kick the ass of any head of state. I think Bill Parcells would have made Saddam Hussein run wind sprints. I think Tom Landry probably should have been president of the United States.

In fact, I think football coaches have all the qualities it takes to run a nation: leadership, toughness, intelligence, and the ability to delegate. Every head coach even has his own little cabinet: Secretary of Special Teams, Chief Justice of the Offensive Line, Majority Leader of the Defense. Imagine how differently Vietnam might have turned out if Vince Lombardi had been running the show instead of Lyndon Johnson; he would have run that toss–counter–sweep right up the Communists' asses. Let's face it: The sixties were a good deal kinder to Lombardi than they were to LBJ. For that matter, the seventies were better to Chuck Noll than they were to Jimmy Carter. In the eighties, Bill Walsh vs. Ronald Reagan was too close to call. I'll give Clinton the nineties over Jimmy Johnson, but not in a runaway, and so far I'll give this decade to Bill Belichick over Bush, but we'll see how it plays out.

The long and short of it is that football coaches command the most important thing in the world: respect. You either respect the coach or you get the hell off the team. It doesn't work that way in other sports. In baseball, it's more important that the manager get along with the players than the other way around; in basketball, the coaches practically deliver room service to the players. But with a football coach, it's my way or the highway. How great it must feel to have that kind of authority.)

The point is, the game ended shortly after I'd stopped crying and then they were interviewing the coach and he was saying that the most important thing in his life is his children. And without thinking, I screamed at the television.

"Bullshit!"

It was purely an impulse, like when the doctor whacks you in the knee with the rubber hammer. I had no control over it. What if that happened when I was on the air? I'd be fired before I got to the next commercial break. My infant girl would be raised on food stamps, and stigmatized as the daughter of the Sportscaster Who Said "Bullshit." Also, beyond any of that, I just can't believe I challenged something a football coach said. That's unprecedented. But it doesn't mean I'm not right.

It *is* bullshit.

You see, I happen to know that coach, and I know he routinely arrives at work at five in the morning and never leaves before eight at night and often sleeps on a sofa in his office. So how many piano recitals is he making it to? How many birthday parties is he missing? I remember Jimmy Johnson once saying he did not make it to the viewing at his own mother's funeral because he was busy preparing for a game; was *his* family the most important thing to him?

Look, this isn't about judging anyone's priorities. If you want to make your job more important than your family, that's not my problem. But don't bullshit yourself that family is your number one priority when clearly it isn't; there are plenty of ways to support a wife and children without sleeping in your office in front of a film projector.

What I don't understand is why none of us have the guts to challenge coaches on stuff like that. When the coach said family is the most important thing in his life, the guy doing the interview gave a nod of appreciation, as though it was wonderful to see such a successful man with his priorities in order. How pathetic is that?

Here's how that interview should have gone:

REPORTER: Congratulations on a great win. How did your team get the job done today?

COACH: Well, we worked hard all week, the coaches did a great job of game planning, and the players went out and executed.

REPORTER: How does it feel to win a big game like this?

COACH: Well, you have to keep things in perspective. When I see my daughters, they aren't going to care that we won or lost—that sort of thing doesn't impress them. They're what really counts.

REPORTER: When's the last time you saw them?

COACH: What do you mean?

REPORTER: I mean, your daughters are four and six years old. Did you see either of them this week?

COACH: Well, I suppose not.

REPORTER: So how exactly do you figure your family is the most important thing?

COACH: Huh?

REPORTER: Do you even remember their names?

(At this point the coach bursts into tears, which he has done publicly only on the day his team won the Super Bowl and he called it the greatest day of his life, overlooking the days his daughters were born.)

COACH: You're right! For God's sake, the other night on the phone I referred to one of them as "the blond one." My whole life is this job! It's all about me, me, me! My family isn't the most important thing in my life, but from this day forward that is going to change!

What would you give to see that interview? Imagine the ratings *that* would get me.

So, what I've decided is that I must be losing my marbles. These are ideas that would *never* have crossed my mind at any other time in my life. I worship football coaches and accept on blind faith every word they say. Now here I am calling out the best coach in the sport for not spending enough time with his kids. I guess I always knew being a father would alter my perspective, but I never imagined it would ruin watching football.

I am going to begin keeping track of my feelings in this journal again, less because I think it helped before than because I often amuse myself by reading it over. And I have nothing to lose. Right now, I'm crying over television commercials. How much lower can I possibly sink than that?

●　　●　　●

Ah, Halloween.

If anything can shake these doldrums—this ridiculous predisposition to laugh, cry, and judge football coaches—it is the smell of carved pumpkins, the taste of marshmallows, and the sound of children shouting, "Trick or treat!"

Halloween was always was my favorite holiday as a boy, as I think it is for most kids. Because a bag filled with candy is worth anything, including wearing the most ridiculous outfit your mother can find in a costume shop. As a boy, my Halloweens were utopian; if they trick-or-treat in heaven, they do it in something that closely resembles an apartment building in Manhattan. That's where I grew up; that's where I did my trick-or-treating. Apartment buildings are the holy land for trick-or-treating: 180 doorbells, no winter coats.

It just doesn't get any better than that.

Actually, my earliest recollection in life, the *very* first thing I remember, took place on Halloween. It involved a lady who lived on the fifth floor of our building, a nasty old woman, a curmudgeon who—in those days—my father called "the spinster." I was six years old the night of that memory, trick-or-treating with a girl friend of mine (not to be confused with "girlfriend") named Sarah Maxwell. She had red hair and freckles, and she wore a wedding dress for a costume; I had on a black leather jacket with my hair slicked back.

I vividly remember the sound of the doorbell (*ka-CHING!*). And I remember the spinster opening her door and looking me over.

"Who are you supposed to be, a criminal?" she asked.

"No," I said. "I'm the Fonz."

She sniffed disapprovingly and dumped a Three Musketeers in my bag. Then she turned to Sarah.

"And you," she said, "what are *you* supposed to be?"

"I'm a beautiful bride."

There was a long pause, followed by a sympathetic sigh.

"You do *look* beautiful, darling," the spinster said. "But, you know, being a bride isn't the only way to *feel* beautiful."

"It isn't?"

"Of course not," the spinster said. "You don't even have to get married if you don't want to."

"I don't?"

"No. When you reach that age and you want to make a decision, you don't even have to choose a man."

"What?"

"There are a number of ways to feel like a woman without being validated by a man. You may even grow to believe that men are the enemy, and if you do, that's okay, too."

"It is?"

"Of course it is," the spinster said. "Now take a Baby Ruth and get out of here."

Then she shut the door in our faces.

I wonder if Sarah Maxwell remembers it.

Anyway, for two decades Halloween lost meaning for me, but then my daughter was born. Now it's back with a vengeance. The first year, we dressed her as a pink flower, in a sweet little getup my mother-in-law sewed. This year was her first time trick-or-treating, dressed as Dorothy the Dinosaur, from the Wiggles. She was excited for the big night, almost as much as I was. Then the trouble began.

You see, I failed to give the most important piece of information at the top of this story: Tonight we trick-or-treated with billionaires.

Living where I do, I am surrounded by others of means and also a select few who have money even we of means cannot comprehend. Like this woman my wife befriended at the gym; she turns out to be married to a fellow who'd made a quick billion running a hedge fund, although, as I was told, "you would never know it."

Frankly, I struggle to see how anyone wouldn't know it when they are greeted at his front door by the butler or when they play the three golf holes in his backyard. Plus, he is colossally pompous. And he feigns listening to my show; which is to say, I am convinced he only turns it on for five minutes when he knows he is going to see me. That way he can always quote something I said, although he never gets the gist of it quite right.

But the billionaires have a daughter about the same age as ours, so it was not unnatural that they invited us to spend Halloween at their home so we could all trick-or-treat together. I was actually looking forward to it, until Mr. Billionaire sent me an e-mail.

Looking forward to seeing you Sunday.
I'll be the one in the Spider-Man suit.
No pictures, please.

I read it four times before I reacted aloud.
"Oh, shit."
There was no mistaking: He was writing to tell me he would be in costume. There was nothing in the world I'd expected less. Was I now supposed to dress in costume just because he was going to? What the hell is the etiquette on this? I'm a thirty-seven-year-old man and I don't have a billion dollars; people will make fun of me to my face if I look ridiculous.

I read the message over and over. There was no other reason he would have written it except to forewarn me that he was dressing up. But why? Was it just so I would not be stunned, or was it to subtly inform me that I, too, was expected to be in costume? I spent the better part of the weekend quizzing every person I came in contact with: Was I obligated to wear a costume for trick-or-treating just because my host was? (And, further, was I making a bigger deal of this than I might have if my host was a cabdriver? Never underestimate the desire to impress a billionaire.)

Ultimately, I decided not to dress up, a decision that was facilitated by the dearth of choices at the costume shop. (I decided that if anyone asked I would say I was dressed as a Metrosexual Sportscaster.) Upon arrival, I was relieved to find that no one but him was dressed as anything but themselves. I felt good about that; even better after the drinks he poured.

Anyway, we just got home. My little girl *loved* trick-or-treating and, I must say, so did I. I even had a good time with the billionaire, and I refuse to hold the costume against him. I may not be the type of dad who dresses up with his kid on Halloween, but I don't want to be the type who makes fun of the dads who do, either. That's not a good type of dad to be. That should be reserved exclusively for nasty old spinsters.

 •   •   •

Let me ask you something: Am I socially obligated to remember the guy who sold me my deck furniture? I don't just mean me—do *you* remember the guy who sold you your deck furniture? And if you don't, should you be made to feel bad about it? I firmly believe you should not, and I say that from the perspective of one who had a perfectly lovely evening ruined because I didn't remember the guy who sold me mine.

Here's what happened: We befriended the Billionaires. After Halloween we were obligated to return their invitation, so we had them to our house. That went well, so then, last night, we were invited to their estate for a spectacular party. I mean fancy. All the beautiful people were there, which is nice, because everybody likes beautiful people.

The dress code was "casual chic," which to the men means "no tie" and to the women means "you will agonize over this decision from the instant you receive the invitation." In that regard it really is an insensitive dress code, but that's the sort of thing you can do when you're a billionaire, because no matter how you dress, everyone will wish they were dressed the same way. If the Billionaires wore matching burlap sacks to a dinner party, no store in town would be able to keep burlap sacks on the shelves the following morning. So, needless to say, there was enormous stress on all the attendees to try to figure out how the Billionaires would dress for their own party. The good news was we knew a few other couples who were going, so my wife was able to synchronize her wardrobe accordingly; none of her friends would be noticeably dressier than the others.

I wore a black cashmere Loro Piana blazer and a silver Prada dress shirt, untucked, with a pair of faded Levi's 501 straight-leg jeans and brown suede Gucci boots. I'd love to tell you that was the first combination I pulled out of my closet. Hell, I'd love to tell you it was among the first ten. The truth is, my wife had insisted upon approval of my outfit and had demanded to see it a full week ahead of time. That way, she'd explained, I would still have time to shop if it didn't meet with her approval. I'd found that a bit demeaning, but at least it took place in private; I saw one guy at the party sent home by his wife for underdressing. (His last words were "What the hell does *casual* mean if I can't wear jeans?")

The place looked sensational, as always, with balloons and strolling guitarists, an enormous buffet supper, and a merengue band. I went straight to the bar. They were pouring top-shelf, so I ordered a Grey Goose martini. Then the music started and a merengue instructor appeared, as if by magic, and took me by the hand. There was no avoiding it; *all* the men were being led onto the dance floor for a merengue lesson.

I handed my wife my drink. "Order me another," I told her. "I'll be right back."

Before I knew it, I was lined up with thirty other white guys, learning the merengue from an effeminate Venezuelan named Jorge. I wanted to laugh at the fellow behind me as he flapped his arms like a chicken, but then I remembered that he'd just sold his company for a hundred million dollars. I also realized that I must look equally bad trying to wiggle my hips like Ricky Martin. I just needed to get the hell out of there, but I couldn't until someone else broke ranks. I danced the best I could until two lawyers on the opposite end headed for the bathroom. I raced behind them and ducked off toward the bar.

As I reclaimed my two drinks from my wife, she said, "You looked cute out there."

I could have just thanked her and left well enough alone, but instead I asked if she really meant it. All she did was smile.

I downed what remained of the first martini in one gulp. "What I think," I said, "is that it is completely inappropriate to force white men to dance."

She sighed. "Isn't Mikhail Baryshnikov white?"

Damn.

Mikhail Baryshnikov is to dancing what Rocky Marciano is to prizefighting: the great white example. There hasn't been a white fighter since Marciano that didn't get his ass kicked, just like Baryshnikov has been the only Caucasian on the dance floor since Fred Astaire hung up the tux. But my argument was destroyed nonetheless. I finished the second drink before dinner was served.

After dessert I was on my way to the bathroom when I was stopped by a guy I recognized but could not place. His face was familiar, but I hadn't a clue why. He just went on and on about the Yankees until the music started and drowned him out. I grabbed another drink before sitting down.

"See that guy?" I said to my wife, nudging her. "In the green jacket."

"Don't point," she answered, without looking up from her dessert.

"There are a hundred people here—how are you going to know who I'm talking about if I don't point?" I asked.

"Just describe him."

By now I had lost him in the crowd. "I think he has short dark hair and a goatee."

"What color eyes?" she asked.

"I don't know what color eyes he has," I said. "Why the hell would I notice the color of his eyes?"

"That guy there." She motioned subtly at exactly the right man.

"That's right," I said. "How did you know who I meant?"

"His eyes are brown," she said. "What about him?"

I explained that I couldn't remember who he was and that it would bother me for the rest of the night if I could not identify him.

"He's the guy who sold us our deck furniture," she said.

That's right! It all came back to me: big Yankee fan, big fan of the show, great deal on the glider. It *was* the guy who'd sold us our deck furniture!

Then my wife went to the bathroom, and on her way back I saw her stop for a chat in a group that included the guy in the green jacket. I went the other way to the bar, because the music was starting again and Jorge was looking for volunteers. I hadn't even taken a sip of my fourth martini when my wife grabbed me from behind. "Deck-furniture guy is bitching about you," she said.

"What?"

"He obviously had no idea who I was," she said, "because he did it right in front of me. He said to some other guy, 'Mister Big Shot Sports Guy over there doesn't even remember me. Some people just think they're so important.' "

"What did you say?" I asked.

"I didn't say anything."

"Thanks for sticking up for me."

"I'm going to dance," she said, and bopped away.

As I drank my fourth martini I started to get aggravated. So what if I didn't remember the guy who'd sold me my deck furniture? Does that make me a bad person? Do all the people he sold deck furniture to remember him three years later? What really rubbed me wrong was him playing the Mister-Big-Shot-Sports-Guy card; that was un-called for. I guarantee that even if I didn't have a radio show, I wouldn't remember the guy who'd sold me my deck furniture.

My wife saw me headed toward him and intercepted me on the way. "It isn't worth it," she said.

She has read and heard so many nasty things about me in my career that she is oblivious to it. (Or maybe she just doesn't care.) I knew she was worried that I would make a scene.

"I'm not going to make a scene," I said. "You know that."

Of course I wasn't. I never make a scene. Not *off* the air, anyway. Instead, I did what I always do: I stewed about it for the rest of the evening.

Then I had the most wonderful dream. In my dream I *did* make a scene. In my dream I walked straight over to the guy in the green jacket and jumped right into his conversation.

"Hey," I said, "aren't you the guy from the deck-furniture store?"

"Yes," he said.

"Sorry I didn't place the face before."

"That's all right," he said, and smirked toward someone in his circle. "I'm sure it happens to you all the time."

In my dream, his condescending tone pissed me off. "No, it does not," I said. "What I do for a living has no bearing on the way I conduct my social relationships. If you and I had one, I can assure you I would have remembered you."

"Well, *I* remembered *you*."

"That's probably because you've seen me on television," I said.

"No, I always remember my customers."

Those were the words I had been waiting for.

"Then why don't you remember my wife?"

I could see the color drain from his face.

"This is my wife," I said, pointing. "She was with me both times we came to the store. She spent more time talking to you than I did."

I loved watching him struggle.

"Who says I didn't recognize her?" he asked.

"I do," I said, stepping closer. "Otherwise you wouldn't have said such nasty things about me in front of her. Now, if you can dig your way out from beneath that hypocrisy, I'll buy beach chairs for everyone in this place."

In the dream, even my wife was impressed. I dreamt that she led every phone conversation the next morning with the deck-furniture story. What a tragedy those things only happen in my dreams. But it did get me thinking. Maybe the answer is to be found in my job. Maybe the answer is to *really* be the guy on the radio. Even when I'm not on the radio.

As I was reading that last episode over just now, what struck me is that it turns out there really *are* pitfalls to being a little famous. Which means I've been wrong all these years. You see, I have always maintained that there is nothing better than being a little famous. And despite what happened at the Billionaires' party, I continue to insist that it is preferable to being very famous or not famous at all.

Here's why: When you are a *little* famous you get nice tables in crowded restaurants. When you are *very* famous you can't go to those restaurants because people bother you. When you are not famous at all you can't even get in, because the owners are afraid you'll bother the famous people.

So being a little famous is great. But in the case of the deck-furniture guy, it screwed me. You see, if I were *very* famous, like Brad Pitt, no deck-furniture salesman would ever expect me to remember him. And if I were not famous at all, the deck-furniture salesman wouldn't care if I forgot him. I suppose the confluence of circumstances really bit me in the ass on that one.

I got bitten again tonight.

This was another evening shot to hell because I am a little famous, another that would have gone much more smoothly if I were either very famous or not famous at all.

We went out for dinner, which we don't do nearly enough, and I always look forward to it. That's why I am so disappointed it went badly. I don't suppose an evening should be expected to pass without a single glitch, but being humiliated three times is a bit much.

It started well: We met our new friends Martin and Lucia at a little Italian place in the neighborhood, just the sort of place I love, a hole in the wall with no attitude and marvelous Italian food. (As much as I enjoy fancy things, to me there is nothing better than *really* good meat sauce. You know the kind: You would eat an old pair of shoes if they came with it.)

I was excited to have the sauce and I was also excited to be with Martin and Lucia. We met them at the Billionaires' party. (Mostly my wife met them; I was in a funk after the deck-furniture incident.)

They are from Italy and their English is flawless but heavily accented; I love that. And, being European, they have cool attitudes. Europeans are infinitely more laid back than Americans. (So laid back, I have no idea when they get any work done. Between the smoking and the napping, I have to think their calendars are pretty full.)

But they make great dinner company.

The moment we sat down the wine was flowing. I allowed Martin to select the wine; I deferred on the strength of his being European. He ordered a bottle of La Valentina Montepulciano d'Abruzzo, which is a damn good bottle of wine from Italy, though, to be honest, I think we'd have all downed it even if it had come from Secaucus. It had been a rough day for all four of us. One spent covered in feces. Literally. Their daughter and our daughter had both had vicious stomach bugs and it had been just brutal; at my house there was no half hour that had passed without a diaper change. Consequently, I would have chugged two glasses before dinner even if the wine had come from a box.

We were all reveling in our shared misery when the first humiliation occurred. It began with two men at a nearby table staring at us, which is nothing unusual. I had no doubt they recognized me, and normally I would have paid it no attention, but I *was* a little bombed and I also had a desire to impress my cool new European friends with how famous I am, so I mentioned it to Martin and Lucia.

"Do you see those guys staring at me?" I motioned as discreetly as a man on two glasses of wine can. "They are obviously fans of my show."

"That's so exciting," Lucia said, in her glorious accent.

We all took turns glancing over indiscreetly, and there was no doubting it—the two guys never stopped looking at our table. Then the waiter came, and before we could order he produced another bottle of wine.

"This is compliments of the two gentlemen over there," he said, pointing to the men we had identified as my fans.

"Oh, that's so nice," I said.

We all raised our glasses toward them and they returned the toast, but showed no sign of approaching our table.

"I guess they don't want to disturb us," I said. "I'll just go over and say thanks."

So I did. I marched straight to their table with a glass of wine in my hand and a big, stupid grin on my face.

"Gentlemen, I just want to say thank you very much. That was very nice and much appreciated, I assure you."

I would love to tell you what they said, but I can't.

Because I don't speak Italian.

The two of them began talking a mile a minute, exclusively in Italian; I don't even know if they were speaking to each other or to me. Eventually, I just walked away. They were still talking when I did; I'm not sure how long it took them to notice I was gone.

When I got back to our table my wife was dipping some gorgeous warm bread into a dish of olive oil.

"Were they nice guys?" she asked between bites.

"They seemed nice," I said. "I don't know."

I was just trying to decide how to explain what happened when it became unnecessary, because they showed up at our table. Then they were speaking Italian with Martin and Lucia, even faster than they had at their own table, only this time my companions joined them and then all four of them were speaking at the same time. I just dipped my bread in the olive oil; there really wasn't anything else to do.

Eventually, Lucia stood up and kissed them both, each on both cheeks, and then they all said "Ciao" and the two guys were gone.

"That was so nice," Lucia said to her husband, in English.

"What did they say?" I asked.

"They recognized this," she said, unwrapping a colorful silk scarf from around her neck. "These scarves are very unique in Italy. You have to come from one tiny little part of the country. They both come from the same town as I do."

"How about that," I said. "What are the odds?"

"And they told me I am the most beautiful woman they have seen on their entire visit to the States."

"Isn't that something," I said. Then, to Martin: "That doesn't bother you at all?"

He smiled. "Of course not."

The sound to my right took me by surprise. I didn't know what it was, at first. Then I realized it was my wife, laughing hysterically. I mean *hysterically*. I have never seen her laugh like that.

"I'm sorry," she said, when she was able to catch her breath. But she didn't stop laughing—she couldn't. Finally, she excused herself and went to the ladies' room. I could still hear the laughter after the door shut behind her.

So instead of impressing my European friends with how famous I am, I made my wife laugh so hard at my expense that she had to pee.

That was the first humiliation.

The second was preferable to the first, if only because at least it was shared. It came about thirty minutes later, after we'd eaten our appetizers and finished the second bottle of wine. Now we were waiting for the pasta, and I had recovered from the first humiliation and was feeling pretty good—or, at least, pretty tipsy.

We were all feeling that way, I guess, and we were talking about the horrors we had encountered all day with our kids. I don't know how much experience you have with babies and diarrhea, but let me assure you, there are few things less pleasant. Talking about it makes you feel better, though, especially with others in the same boat. Parents of young children often engage in lengthy discussions about their children's feces. Now the four of us were sharing a laugh over it and discussing in excruciating detail the size, color, consistency, clarity, odor, texture, and volume of the crap we had dealt with all day.

We were having a lovely time, but I could not help but notice that the couple seated at the table next to ours kept looking at us. Once again, I was sure it was one of my fans, but there was no way in hell I was going to say anything about it. I just ignored him, no matter how obviously he looked at me, and we all just went on talking and laughing and drinking. Then, just as the waiter emerged from the kitchen with our food, the man at the table next to ours—the one who'd been staring—leaned closer and spoke.

"Excuse me, but would you people mind?" he snapped. "We are trying to eat."

Instantly, we were all silent. While we *are* parents, we are also people of good manners and reasonable breeding; we all know it is rude to discuss dirty diapers loudly at the dinner table.

"You have completely ruined our evening," said the woman.

That was the second humiliation. And there's no doubt it left a damper on our group. We all ate quietly; even the meat sauce didn't seem so special.

I'm sure we were all relieved when the couple paid their check and rose to leave. I buried my face in my pasta bowl as they shuffled past. All I could think was: At least it's over.

"And by the way," the guy said, as he passed, "I'm going to tell everyone what a disgusting slob the Metrosexual Sportscaster really is."

That was the third humiliation. Of all the people to recognize me in front of my cool European friends, it had to be the one guy who admonished our etiquette.

I was still down when we got home, but my wife quickly started laughing again over the guys who'd sent the wine. She bounces back from humiliations faster than I do. All I know is, I *really* needed a fun night out and I didn't get to have one.

As I climb into bed now and open this journal I can hear her washing up—she's still laughing. I guess I'm glad she's in such a good mood. I wonder if it will last into tomorrow. I also wonder if my daughter is over her stomach virus. And most of all I wonder, What the hell did we used to talk about over dinner before we were up to our foreheads in feces?

•   •   •

Wow, celebrity really *is* a strange phenomenon.

This is obviously becoming a recurring topic, but only because things keep happening to reinforce it. First the deck-furniture guy, then the ruination of my meat sauce, and now this most recent episode, which was really over the top.

It began yesterday, when I was idly flipping through the channels and came across *The Ellen DeGeneres Show.* I happen to like Ellen DeGeneres, but yesterday she had on some actress I could not place who was going on and on about how much she loves her dog. And if that wasn't tedious enough, Ellen then pulled out a picture of the dog and displayed it for the cameras, and the entire studio audience sighed in unison, one of those syrupy sighs you only hear on talk shows.

This for a German shepherd.

Now, let's make one thing perfectly clear: There is nothing cute about a German shepherd. The dog is not meant to be cute; it is the closest thing the animal world has to a Nazi. No German shepherd is worthy of a group sigh. This dog got one only because our society is so completely obsessed with celebrity. Any member of that studio audience who came across that dog in the street would run like hell, but when a B-level actress says she loves it, suddenly it's like she donated a kidney.

I can only imagine the comments later, when the actress went into the crowd to sign autographs.

"I just loved that dog! It is so wonderful that someone like you finds time to care for a pet."

"That dog was the cutest thing I have ever seen. I'm going to get one of my own this weekend."

"A German shepherd chewed off my Uncle Herman's leg, but now that I know you have one I've decided I love them, too."

All that for an actress who came on *after* the stand-up comic.

But the thing is, it happens all the time. It even happens to me.

People tell me how wonderful it is that I spend time with my daughter. What is so wonderful about it? Don't you spend time with your kids? My life is anything but glamorous, but even if it were I shouldn't be commended for not trashing a hotel suite or banging an intern.

Famous people are no different from anyone else. They wake up with the same yellow crap in the corner of their eyes and they get the same gassy stomach after eating chili peppers. Their lives aren't airbrushed just because their photos are.

This goes for sports as much as any other form of entertainment. The adoration bestowed upon star athletes is an embarrassment, but do not make the mistake of blaming the celebrities for that; the fault lies not with our stars but with us. All the money, all the adoration, all the pampering—that comes from us. It is easy to blame the media or the marketers, but if *you* choose to wait in line for seven hours to get a baseball signed, don't blame the signer if he develops an inflated sense of self-importance.

That's where Bo Jackson comes in.

For all the famous athletes I've covered, including the years I spent with Michael Jordan, the most up-close view I ever got of what it means to be enormously famous was with Bo.

And it wasn't pretty.

This was when Bo was playing baseball with an artificial hip. He had the surgery after suffering from a debilitating disease that would eventually deprive him of his football career and deprive the rest of us of seeing the greatest athlete of our time. You can have anyone else you want; I'll take Bo Jackson as the greatest pure athlete ever. In fact, I think if he had stayed healthy he could have been the greatest running back ever to play in the NFL while also being an all-star-caliber baseball player and—if he had found the time—an Olympic decathlete, too. There may never have been a more gifted athlete, in our time or any other.

He was also a cultural superstar because of the brilliant Nike marketing campaign centered around his name. If you're old enough, you certainly remember the "Bo knows" commercials, including the great one with the legendary guitarist of the same name saying, "Bo, you don't know Diddley."

After Bo Jackson had surgery on his hip he could no longer play football, but he did make a short-lived baseball comeback, becoming the only man ever to compete in a major professional sport with an artificial hip. That was when I covered him, when he was playing for the White Sox, still among the biggest stars in the world but a shell of his former self on the field. It was more sad than it was inspiring to watch him limp about, and I got the sense he was sad, too; he was sullen and withdrawn most of the time, and his naturally introverted personality didn't help.

Then came one day, late in the 1993 season, when the White Sox were on the verge of clinching a division championship. I traveled with them to Oakland and stayed in the team hotel, which is how I found myself on a shuttle bus, headed to the stadium, with only Bo Jackson and me on board.

I wasn't excited about it at first; I was already over the thrill of being close to very famous people and, frankly, Bo was a man of few words and almost none were worth hearing. But as we pulled into the stadium parking lot and I watched the masses descend upon us, I grew quite excited. Maybe *excited* isn't the right word; I was scared out of my mind.

I don't know how to begin to describe the bedlam. Until security arrived it was utter chaos. I remember one woman in particular—she couldn't have been older than twenty—with her face pressed against the bus window in sickening fashion, unable to pull away for the crush behind her.

I turned to Bo. "Is it always like this?" I asked.

He didn't respond, didn't even nod. I don't know if he was too shocked to speak or just so accustomed to the havoc that he didn't even notice.

"What is it like to have this all the time?" I asked.

He turned to me then, and looked me up and down. He was among the most famous and dynamic ballplayers in the world, but at that moment he could not have appeared less powerful. Mostly, he just looked tired. Then he sighed, and I can still feel the weight of that sigh.

"My man," he said, as the uniformed personnel cleared space so our bus could pull away from the throng, "you could never understand unless you walked a mile in my shoes."

I remember thinking that I would never want to, and I still feel that way today. Not for all his talent and all his money.

That brings us back to yesterday, when, after watching Ellen DeGeneres, I went out to buy a Village People CD. That may sound like an odd thing to do, but not if you have seen my daughter dance to the song "Y.M.C.A." She does all the arm motions and shouts out the lyrics at the top of her lungs. She loves it, so it occurred to me that she might enjoy other songs by the Village People as well. (You see, I remember "Y.M.C.A." before it became an arena staple, and I didn't even think it was the best of their songs. I preferred "Macho Man" and "In the Navy" and "Go West.")

So I went to Tower Records and I was standing in line, lost in my memories of sixth-grade dance contests, when a voice came from behind me.

"Hey, aren't you the guy from the radio?"

"Yeah."

"I love the show," the guy said.

He immediately began describing how he had hooked his whole family on listening to me, and how he hates Howard Stern, and how much he loves the Yankees, and he related his vividly detailed recollection of the first ball game his father took him to.

Then he asked me a simple question. "So, what are you buying?"

I just held up the CD. He looked a little startled, and I guess I couldn't blame him. He had just come across the guy he listens to on the radio every morning buying *The Best of the Village People*. I suppose that isn't an everyday occurrence.

I mumbled a "best of luck" and went to the register to pay my fifteen bucks. By the time I got home I had forgotten all about that guy; I was just excited to watch my daughter dance to "Macho Man."

Then I got to work this morning and all hell had broken loose.

"Where were you yesterday?" my producer asked accusingly.

"What do you mean?"

"You're all over the message boards," he said. "Were you in a gay porn shop?"

"What the hell are you talking about?"

He handed me a stack of paper, printouts from websites and Internet chat rooms, all talking about me.

"Where were you yesterday?" he asked again.

"Nowhere," I said. "I was here most of the afternoon."

And then it hit me. Tower Records. A self-described metrosexual wearing Prada and buying *The Best of the Village People*.

"This is ridiculous," I said.

"You're going to have to address it on the air," my producer said.

"No I'm not," I said, and I didn't. I did my show exactly the way I had intended to and I never once looked at all the e-mail. Then my cell phone rang on my way home.

"Michael, what the hell is going on?"

"I don't know, Aunt Ada," I said. "That depends on what you mean."

"Fern Cohen is offering even money that you're gay and your marriage is just a front," she said. "She never moves a line like this unless she has inside information. Is there something you aren't telling me, darling?"

For the first time in my life, I hung up on my aunt. And as I drove the rest of the way home, I started to feel as though I *had* walked in Bo Jackson's shoes. Maybe not a mile, but at least a few steps. And, for a little while, I think I understood.

●　　　●　　　●

Well, I guess today was a pretty good reminder that there are things much tougher about my job than being embarrassed by strangers or called out by a deck-furniture salesman. The really hard part is when the show becomes personal. Like this morning, when that lady called.

It happened early, which is especially bad because it threw me off for the rest of the morning. And it began so innocently, too. I was casually riffing on how the only reason to watch the Olympics was the outfits on the women's beach volleyballers (you know, those bathing suits you could floss with) and I got egged on and wound up saying things that may have been closer to the sexist line than I usually go. But everyone was loving it. My staff was laughing, I was laughing. It was good radio.

Then a woman I've never met ruined it.

Her name was Celia; she was calling from Brooklyn. "Greeny," she said, in a disappointed tone, "how would you feel if people talked about your daughter like that?"

I froze. Then I tried to pass it off as funny, but I don't think that went over. The show had a decidedly dead feel after that. This is tough territory for a guy who is closer to a feminist than a misogynist and, more important, a dad. I don't want my daughter to hear me talk like that on her way to school. Do Howard Stern's daughters listen to *his* show? I wonder how he deals with that.

My daughter is growing up in a culture that provides her with more opportunities than any previous generation had. Her grandmother was the first woman in our family to go to college, and her mother has a master's degree. My daughter could be president someday. That's the way change works. Not day to day or year to year; real change is made generation to generation. Take sports, for example: When I was a kid, I didn't even know there *was* women's college basketball. Now it is enormously popular and there is professional basketball for women, too. I have no reason to believe that my little girl will be athletic, or even that she'll gravitate to sports at all, but I'm glad she'll know it's there if she wants it.

When I was growing up, I was aware of only three female athletes.

(Discounting the Olympians who came and went in the flash of two weeks and were never heard from again.) There was Chris Evert, Billie Jean King, and Martina Navratilova. And the reality is, I was aware of each of them only for the ways they related to men.

I knew Chrissie because every man loved her.

I knew Billie Jean because she beat a man.

And I knew Martina because she seemed like a man.

(That alone is evidence of how far this has come. We thought Martina was masculine because she rushed the net. If we had seen the muscles on Serena Williams or Amelie Mauresmo back then, we probably would have called the cops.)

Looking back, how sad it is that female athletes were accessible only in the way they related to men. It is a wonder that Mia Hamm and Diana Taurasi came along at all. They were products of that era; who were *their* role models? Whose posters did they have on their walls? I am going to buy posters of female athletes and put them up in my daughter's room; I'm doing it today. She is almost two years old. I hope I'm not too late.

Opening Monologue

The following day

I bought my daughter some posters this week. I bought her some athletes so she can have them on her wall. I bought her Derek Jeter and Chad Pennington and Anna Kournikova.

I can already hear the women screaming at me in their cars. "Kournikova? Are you kidding me? Why not just buy her the poster of a porn star? Don't you know she's more famous for her looks than her game? Why would you pick Kournikova, of all the women in sports?"

I'll tell you why.

Because sex sells.

The reality is, my daughter is going to grow up wanting to be considered pretty. All girls do; why wouldn't she? She is also going to want to be considered sexy. And you know what? I hope she thinks: I want to look just like Anna.

Have you ever really looked at Anna Kournikova? She is a jock. She is a beautiful woman, no question, but she is also a jock. She has big, athletic shoulders and muscular arms and legs; a generation ago she would have been considered manly. But now she is considered sexy, and she is. And I'll tell you something else she is that is infinitely more important.

She is healthy.

You don't get to look like she does by making yourself throw up after you eat. You don't look like she does if you were on Weight Watchers at age nine. And you don't look like she does if your diet consists solely of black coffee, cigarettes, egg whites, and Ecstasy. That's *not* how you grow up to look like Anna Kournikova. To look like Anna you've got to eat—a lot—and healthily. And you've got to work out. I don't mean an hour on the treadmill, I mean lifting weights and dedicating yourself to physical fitness. How much better off will my little girl be if *that* is what she thinks is sexy? How much better off would yours be?

If you think it is a better idea that our daughters think Jennifer Aniston is sexy, then you can get a poster of her. I can't deny that I think she is sexy, too. But she is also skinny. *Really* skinny. The kind of skinny that looks like a sandwich would send her system into shock; the kind of skinny where if someone on the set breaks wind she gets blown into a wall; the kind of skinny where if you took away the fancy clothes you could generate donations for a hunger charity based on her photos. That's how skinny Jennifer Aniston is. You don't get that skinny by being healthy. You get that skinny by not eating.

So I'm going to put the Anna Kournikova poster on my daughter's wall and maybe later I'll get Mia Hamm and Serena Williams and Maria Sharapova or whatever women follow in their footsteps. Women who aren't only great athletes but beautiful, too. Because the chances of my daughter being a great athlete are pretty slim, but the chances of her wanting to look like one are pretty good.

And that could save her life.

And while I'm on the subject, I'm not going to stop talking about how pretty some of the female athletes are, either. Why should I? It doesn't mean I don't appreciate their athleticism; it just means I am a normal person. Why do so many women name Derek Jeter as their favorite ballplayer? Because of the way he pivots on the double play? Of course not. It's because he's a good-looking guy, and there isn't anything wrong with that, either.

So don't call me up and tell me I should protect our daughters by keeping the subjects of sports and sex separate. In the long run, I am doing them the biggest favor I possibly can.

● ● ●

A lot of people really liked what I said about my daughter on the radio. Others didn't. That's okay; I'm used to it. People rarely agree on things. Today, however, after I told them what I said to my daughter *last* night, the feeling was unanimous.

I am a disgrace.

In my own defense, I have hardly been sleeping at all lately. I've been up with my daughter almost every night because my wife has been traveling. The exhaustion is starting to take a toll on my work, too; yesterday I called Shaquille O'Neal "Tatum." That's a mistake you're only allowed to make once.

Anyway, my wife finally came back, so when I got into bed last night I turned on *her* baby monitor rather than my own. Then I slept, hard. I was having the loveliest dream, too: Elizabeth Hurley presented me with an Academy Award and then I was at the after-party with Steven Tyler and Chelsea Clinton. I'm not even sure that would be fun, but I'll never know because just then I was awakened by the tapping of a two-year-old girl.

This wasn't the dream anymore.

"Daddy, I'm all wet."

As my eyes adjusted I could see the stain on her pajamas; they were soaked. My daughter just moved from a crib into a big-girl bed. She is really excited about the move. Just now, I'm not.

"It's all right, sweetie, there's nothing to be upset about."

She was holding back tears. "Daddy, my bed is all wet."

I had two options. I could take her back to her room, change her into dry pajamas, strip the bed, put dry sheets on, and get her back to sleep—a twenty-minute commitment, minimum—or I could pull her into bed beside me, where she would fall asleep instantly. Of course, if I went with plan B, I would be soaked in pee.

Tough decision.

Then a third option entered my mind. I don't know how it did, and I don't know why. I just know that once it was there, I could not fight it.

"Sweetie, why don't you get into bed with Mommy," I said. "She's been away so much that she's missed you. She would love for you to sleep with her."

The look on my baby's face was worth a million dollars. She ran around the other side of the king-sized bed and snuggled up next to my wife. Now I was fifteen seconds from glory. If she fell asleep without waking my wife up, no one would be the wiser until I was long gone, at work. I counted backward in my head. When I got to zero I heard my daughter's breathing steady off. My wife never budged. I had pulled it off. I drifted back to sleep and awoke at my usual time, feeling the most rested I have in a month.

I would have gotten away with all of it if I'd tried to. The only reason I got found out is that I gave myself away in the interest of ratings. Simply put, it's a good story and I got egged into telling it on the air. The reaction from my audience was about what you would expect. America has decided I am a disgusting slob.

I was in a great mood when the phone rang in the car on my way home.

"Michael, I hear your marriage is breaking up."

"What? Who is this?"

"Who do you think it is, Lainie Kazan?"

Only my Aunt Ada could come up with Lainie Kazan.

"What makes you think my marriage is breaking up?"

"What do you think I am, out of the loop?" she asked. (Always— a question with a question.) "Something about the little one peeing on your wife."

"Ada, it's a story I told on the radio. It has nothing to do with my marriage."

"Do you not realize I was married for almost eleven months?" she scolded. "I know from marriages breaking up. And I know that when you instruct your daughter to urinate on your wife, it's just a question of time."

"Aunt Ada, my marriage is fine."

"Now, you listen to me," she said, "I can get an over/under of six months from Fern Cohen, so you call me before you file anything."

"Fern Cohen has an over/under on my marriage?"

"She does, and I'm already into her two grand from the World Series," my aunt said. "She holds that over my head every Tuesday night. I *need* this, Michael."

"I can't believe she's predicting my marriage will break up in six months."

"She had the line at one year," she said. "But after that story this morning she moved it."

"Aunt Ada, are you asking me to get divorced so you can win a bet?"

"Of course not," she said. "You should be ashamed of yourself for suggesting such a thing. All I'm saying is, if you're going to get divorced anyway, why shouldn't I make a few bucks on it?"

"I guess I can see that."

"Good, darling. Are you eating? On television you look thin."

"I'm feeling fine, Ada."

"That's good, how are the little ones?"

"They're great. Actually just yesterday—"

"Honey, I have to go, the police are here."

"What? Why are the police there?"

"It's a long story, darling," she said. "Now, do me a favor. If you don't hear from me by the end of the week, have someone pick up Jimmy the Greek at the vet."

"What?"

"He's being fixed. I love you, darling, best to the family."

And she was gone.

Jimmy the Greek is her dog, a tiny white bulldog with a face that looks like it's smushed up against a glass door. It must be ten years old, maybe more. I don't know much about dogs, but I'm pretty sure you normally get them fixed earlier than that.

With nothing else to do I gave my mother a call. She's usually good for a little griping on the insanity of our family, but there would be none of that today. And I should have seen it coming, because it took five rings before she answered. That's always trouble.

"Michael, I just disconnected your father, hold on."

There was a click and a long silence. Then a dial tone. The woman has never jumped from one call to another without cutting someone off. Usually, she disconnects both calls. If she maintains contact with either, it's a moral victory.

I dialed again.

"Hello?" she answered, still flustered.

"Ma, it's me."

"Michael, please don't call when I'm on the other line," she said.

"How am I supposed to know when you're on the other line?"

"Call me back later," she said, and hung up.

When I got home, there was an e-mail waiting.

Re: phone calls
Don't call before noon, your father calls then sometimes.
Also in the afternoon. Try before dinner.

Less than twenty minutes later, another came.

Re: quick question
Yes, I do. You are a good son to think of your father, it could save his life.

That was all.

The print was blue, which means she was replying to something I had asked. But whatever that was, she had erased it. So now I am trying to remember what question I asked my mother, and I am in turmoil because whatever it is may save my father's life. My options are to risk calling again to ask or leave it alone and hope it doesn't kill my father. Those are the kinds of decisions we make in my family.

I take comfort in knowing that my mother's idea of what may kill my father is almost unlimited. Once she said it would kill him if he did not wear a jacket on a cool night. Another time she accused *me* of attempted murder for encouraging him to order a sour pickle. It is a miracle he has survived into his seventies.

I think I'm just going to ignore the e-mail and hope nothing terrible happens. And in the event it does, I'm hopeful it will take her so long to reach me that she'll forget it was my fault. Most of all, I'm just looking forward to another good night's sleep. Those have been hard to come by lately.

● ● ●

Perhaps a business trip is the best thing for my troubled mind right now. With everything that's been going on, I feel like two days of wiping no one's behind but my own could be just what I need.

I'm in Houston, where I arrived in the afternoon and had a dinner that went late into the evening. I got back to the hotel tired and tipsy, and the wake-up call was only six hours away. But as I lay on the bed, I flipped on the TV anyway. I find I can't fall asleep without the television when I'm not with my wife, which is ironic because when I'm home and she wants to watch television, it keeps me awake. The equation seems to be as follows:

Wife + television = no sleep
No wife + no television = no sleep
Wife + no television = sleep
No wife + television = porn

I would guess every man knows that lonely feeling of flipping through the channels, hoping to find something that has the potential for nudity. In hotels now they have made it too easy; it's almost impossible not to sample the erotica. Often I don't even intend to, but the hotel people are tricky—they put that menu on the screen immediately and that sexy silhouette pops up. At that point, even if you had no intention of watching porn, you can't help but be tempted. So you select the option and they present the movie choices with sexy photos and brief descriptions.

TEENAGE TWATS

We dispatch with any pretense of a plot and get right to the action. These girls all have two things in common: tight butts and a desire to lose their virginity. Limited dialogue allows for plenty of action. Featuring girl-on-girl and a wild ménage that leaves everyone exhausted but satisfied.

Movie titles do not appear on hotel receipt.

That last line is the one that gets me. I wonder how many traveling salesmen handed in expense reports that said *Teenage Twats*, before the hotels got the idea. But, really, who is fooled by this? Does anyone believe that a business traveler decided to settle down at eleven o'clock at night to watch eight minutes of *Seabiscuit*?

Anyway, enough about the porn.

Something much more significant has happened on this trip, something far more worthy of discussion and, no doubt, consternation: I've come to the realization that I'm getting old.

That's a much bigger deal than getting *older*. We are all getting *older*, at the same exact pace; some of us have just been at it longer than others. I'm getting *old*. That means I've been getting older for a really long time.

This realization came to me somewhat gradually on the trip down here. It began on the plane, when I was reading *The New York Times*. I found a story saying there is concern about sexual activity on school buses. It seems schoolgirls are performing oral sex upon schoolboys, and the parents are hysterical. One of them described the situation as "a tragedy."

Of course, I agree.

It was not until later that I started to think about just how far removed from those boys I have become. I used to ride the school bus, and back then I couldn't find a girl willing to let me feel her up. But I think if I *had* ever received oral sex on the school bus my head would have exploded. Thus, I guarantee you the boys on that bus today don't consider this a tragedy. They probably consider it the greatest thing ever to happen in the history of education.

So, when exactly did this transformation in *me* take place? When did I go from being one of those boys to whatever it is I am now? I need to spend some time thinking about that. Don't let me forget to do so.

The following day (still in Houston)

When I finished the show this morning I was still thinking about being old and it sort of bummed me out, so I decided to cheer myself up with ice cream. There was a Ben & Jerry's down the street, so I walked over, alone. A bunch of teenagers were hanging around in front of the ice-cream store, riding skateboards and smoking cigarettes, just as I did when I was their age. Sometimes I identify with those kids. In my mind, I am still one of them.

Then I found myself doing a little dance with one of them, one of those awkward face-to-faces where whichever way *you* go, *he* goes, and vice versa. Finally, he stepped back with a little smile and said: "You go ahead, sir."

I stopped dead in my tracks.

Sir?

That one word had more meaning than most books. It said, "Dude, you're not one of us anymore. You're one of them. And if we smoke a joint later, you're the one we're going to be hiding it from."

And the tragedy is, he's right. I'm *not* one of them anymore. Not just because of my age; I simply don't understand young people today. I can't relate to the piercing or the tattoos, I don't understand why their pants begin below their hips, and I *definitely* don't get the music. All I hear on FM radio today is noise, which is ironic because my father thought *my* music was noise and I'm sure his father felt the same way. Maybe the kids who grew up in the eighteenth century listening to Mozart heard the same complaints from their parents.

"I don't know how you listen to this Mozart. That concerto is pure noise. In my day we had Bach. Now, that was music."

I guess it all comes down to what you are accustomed to. Bach and Mozart are, for most of us, indistinguishable by era, but only because so much time has passed. Two hundred years from now, the Beatles and Pearl Jam will be thought of as contemporaries. So will Louis Armstrong and Puffy Combs. As laughable as it may seem, there are actually greater similarities between Michael Jackson and Eminem than there are between Bach and Mozart; only time has blurred the line. So despite all the fathers who grew up on Louis Armstrong telling their kids that P. Diddy is nothing but noise, someday the two may very well be considered interchangeable.

I guess the point is that some feelings are timeless. There have always been old farts and young whippersnappers, and there always will be. The interesting part for me is that I used to be just one of them. Now I'm starting to think I may be both.

If there is any good news to be found in my advancing age, it is that I don't believe I am growing cynical. Hopeless, perhaps, but not cynical. By that, I mean I do not believe that my degree of cynicism has increased. Instead, I've just become acutely aware of my complete inability to effect change.

Here it is in a nutshell:

When I was younger, I thought: This is bullshit.

Now I think: This is bullshit, and there isn't a damn thing I can do about it.

The world is becoming a smaller and smaller place for me, which makes no sense, because you should learn more and more about it as you grow. But what is actually happening to me is I am realizing that the overwhelming majority of the world's problems don't make a bit of difference in my life. For example, I *do* have empathy for endangered species in Antarctica—I really do—but I would sacrifice one or two in a heartbeat if it would keep my cable from going out so often.

If that seems trivial, that's the point. I have come to see the important stuff replaced in stature by the minutiae. So, while I do side with striking autoworkers, I would be a good deal more interested in their cause if just once one of them would offer to pick up my dry cleaning. Sometimes I think those feelings make me a shallow, self-centered, narcissistic bastard. But most times I think they just make me human.

After the ice-cream break there was lunch with contest winners, which means I got paid to sit in a restaurant and talk sports with one lucky listener and eleven of his friends. The drive to the restaurant took forever, and at some point I realized what was going on, where we were going, and my brain beheld two words you never want to hear:

Outside Houston.

As the limo made its way through whatever godforsaken town we wound up in, every person I saw was packing heat. Which wasn't surprising, since every store was a gun shop. It went pretty much like this: Exxon station, gun store, Arby's, gun store, Red Lobster, post office, gun store. (The proximity of the post office struck me as particularly off-putting; too easy for the disgruntled postal worker to make himself dangerous.)

When we finally arrived at the restaurant I found the contest winner seated with his wife and three other men. They were all dressed in identical camouflage. Even the wife. It looked like a scene from *Platoon*. (I couldn't decide who looked more ridiculous, the woman in the camouflage or me in an Etro shirt and Gucci loafers.)

It was quickly explained that they had all just come from the range.

"That's funny," I said. "I've been playing golf all my life and never seen anyone dressed like this."

When the laughter subsided I found out I was in the company of the Texas state champion Clay Pigeon Shooting Club. They were Clay Pigeon shooters, all of them, including the woman; she was team captain and female state champion seven years running. She had been shooting since she was a little girl and had met her husband, now seated to her left, on the night of their high school prom when neither of them had much felt like dancing so they stole away to the shooting range together.

I'm not making this up.

"Were you wearing a prom dress?" I asked.

She nodded.

"You in a tux?" I asked him.

He smiled. "Better believe it."

"Camouflage?" I asked.

"Nope," he said. "They didn't make them back then."

Change the subject.

"So, do you eat the pigeons?"

They all laughed at me again and then explained that clay pigeons are not edible. They aren't even birds; they're made of clay.

"Are they shaped like pigeons?" I asked.

"Not really," the woman said.

"Then why are they called pigeons?"

They all seemed at a loss, so I excused myself and went to the bathroom while they waited for the others to arrive. When I returned the guy across the table from me—Andy—seemed eager to strike up a conversation. I did the best I could.

"You always been from around here?" I asked, dropping the auxiliary verb to sound more authentic.

"Born here, raised here, figure I'm gonna die here," Andy said.

"I'm from New York," I said.

"What part of New York?"

"Manhattan."

"That's New York City?" he asked.

"Yup."

"Right *in* New York City?"

"That's right."

Andy looked stunned. "Let me ask you about something," he said. "It is my understanding that the motor vehicles in New York City do not come equipped with air-conditioning."

(I loved the way he said "vehicles," with the emphasis on the second syllable. It came out vee-HICKLES.)

"I'm sorry, what?" I asked.

"In your experience, do the motor vehicles in New York City come equipped with air-conditioning?"

"Many people in New York don't have cars," I said, "but every one I've ever been in has had air-conditioning."

"Interesting," Andy said.

Not really.

But then a really interesting thing *did* happen.

All the buddies we were waiting for came in the door together, and everyone was shaking hands and hugging, and three of them were black. I was being introduced to a bunch of people whose names I would never remember and all I could do was stare in stunned silence at the black ones. They too were members of the shooting team, so they were dressed in camouflage and spoke like characters out of *Deliverance*, just like the others. But, again, they were black.

While everyone was ordering I had a moment to consider the fact that these rednecks are obviously a hell of a lot more open-minded than I am. The notion that they might have black friends shocked me, but of course it didn't faze them a bit. Clearly the only presuppositions at that table were being made by me. If anyone was prejudiced, it wasn't the rednecks—it was the bleeding-heart liberal from New York.

So I suppose I learned two valuable lessons on this trip. The first is: No matter what you think, the world sees you for what you are. And the second is: No matter how much Prada and Armani you own, never assume that you know more than the guy in the camouflage tux.

●　　●　　●

In the last forty-eight hours, my wife has been speaking to me for only three minutes. But for what it's worth, they were the three best minutes of the weekend.

It began Saturday morning when the phone rang too early. I answered and was surprised to hear the familiar voice of my friend Harvey, a doctor I know mostly through football; we've been attending games together for years.

"Leslie left," he said.

Leslie was his wife of ten years, the most passionate female football fan I have ever met.

"What do you mean?" I asked.

"She's gone," he said. "Packed her bags, said there's someone else . . ."

His voice drifted off. I sat in silence, painfully aware of how tired I was.

"She left me," he said.

I didn't know what to say, so I didn't say anything. But then he didn't say anything either, and it became uncomfortable.

"Are we still going to the game tomorrow?" I asked.

"I guess so. She didn't take the tickets," he said.

"All right," I said. "I'll see you there."

I lay back and stared at the ceiling. They didn't have kids, and I supposed that was for the best. They had met in the stands at a Jets game and hadn't missed a game in years. In truth, I hardly knew them outside of football, but the games have been such a big part of our lives that I consider them among my closest friends.

What a shame.

I was just going back to sleep when I discovered my wife staring a hole through me.

"I'm sorry he called so early," I said. "Try to go back to sleep."

"Are you kidding me?"

"What?"

"I'm not upset that he woke us up," she said. "I could hear the entire conversation."

"Oh."

"His wife just left him!"

"I know," I said.

"Are you telling me you have no idea why I'm upset right now?"

"As a matter of fact I don't," I said, now resigned to staying awake. "You barely know them."

"Let's retrace our steps here, shall we?"

"I wish we wouldn't. I hate retracing our steps."

But it was useless. She was going to retrace, no matter how tired I was.

"Your friend called you at six in the morning to tell you his wife left him," she said. "And what did you say?"

I thought about it. Suddenly I couldn't recall if I'd said anything at all.

"You said, and let me quote you: Are we still going to the game tomorrow?"

"Yeah."

"So what happened is that your friend called to say his wife left him and you asked if he was still going with you to the football game."

When she said it like that, it sounded different from how it had felt when it happened.

"What was I supposed to say?" I asked.

"How about that you're so sorry his wife left him?"

"I really believe that goes without saying."

She put her hands over her eyes. "How about asking if there is anything you can do to help?"

"I hate when people say that," I said. "His wife just left him. What am I going to do, pick up his dry cleaning?"

"You could just offer to help," she said. "That's what people do."

"I understand that, so long as you understand that people are making an empty offer knowing it won't amount to anything. The best thing I can do is take him to the football game tomorrow to get his mind off it."

"You are impossible."

"I'm impossible?" I asked.

"That's correct."

With that, she was gone. A minute later I heard the shower and quickly began to focus on the real issue at hand. With our schedules as they are, Saturday mornings are usually the best chance we have for a little fooling around. And suddenly that was looking like a very slim possibility.

Immediate reconciliation was my only hope. I went into the bathroom, where the steam was just beginning to show on the mirrors. "I'm going to call him back in a little while," I shouted. "I'll give him some time, then maybe take a run out to his house this afternoon."

She didn't say anything for a minute, then pushed open the shower door and beckoned me with a finger. What a relief.

Three minutes later I was back in the bedroom, staring at the phone. "I'm going to call now," I shouted.

"I'm proud of you," she replied from the bathroom.

I was waiting to hear the hair dryer. My best shot at coming out of this unscathed was if she didn't hear the phone call. Once she started the blow dryer I would have a good ten minutes of relative privacy. But it never went on. Soon she emerged wearing a baseball cap. I usually love the way she looks in a baseball cap. Not this time.

"Are you going to call?" she asked. "I'm hungry."

"We could eat first," I said. "I can call later."

"Call him now, you know he's awake," she said.

I sighed inwardly and picked up the phone. I could hear the surprise in his voice when he answered.

"What's up?" he asked.

"Nothing," I said. "I just wanted to see if there was anything I could do for you."

"Like what?" he laughed.

I looked over at the wife and remembered she could hear both ends of the conversation. I reminded myself to do something about the volume on that blasted phone.

"Well," I said, hesitantly, "do you want me to see if I can get someone to use her ticket?"

The door to my bedroom had slammed before he could answer.

"Actually, I thought we'd leave her seat open, at least this week," he said.

"Whatever you want, man," I said.

"All right, see you tomorrow."

"See you."

When I got downstairs, my wife wasn't speaking to me. I tried to explain that I *was* agreeing to leave the seat empty, even though I thought it seemed like a complete waste, but she didn't want to hear it. With nothing else to do, I went to the gym. On the treadmill, I thought a little more about the entire fiasco. First off, what purpose was being served by leaving an empty chair? This wasn't a seder, it was a football game. Why should there be less support for the team just because a marriage had fallen apart? Then I got around to the unfairness of the persecution I was suffering. She wants me to offer help, but then she doesn't like the help I offer. How am I supposed to win? It seems my only hope is to ask her what to do *and* how to do it. Otherwise, there will be a lot more silent weekends.

The following day

The nightmarish postscript to this disaster is that the Jets lost and a fan of the opposing team wound up in the seat we had left vacant, heckling us the entire afternoon. On the way home I asked Harvey how he was feeling and he said, "All things considered, this was worse than yesterday." Then I asked if there was anything I could do and he told me to shut the fuck up. I'm going to tell my wife he said that. I hope she sees the humor in it. I'm not sure she will.

Surrender

Opening Monologue
December 18, 2001

I received a very nice invitation today.

I was invited to come watch the opening ceremonies of the Olympics in Salt Lake City. They are coming up, you know. Just a few months away, right here in our country.

Pretty soon the first medals will be awarded, and the big questions will be asked: Who will emerge as the star of these games?

Who will capture the imagination of the American people?

Who will move the most boxes of cereal?

Isn't that what it has really boiled down to? Who winds up on the next box of Wheaties? Isn't that sad? Somewhere deep inside, doesn't that make you ache?

It does me. That's why I politely declined the invitation.

Because the Olympics have become a sham.

It kills me to say that. It makes me feel discouraged and sad.

As a sports fan and as a parent. And I'll tell you why. Because my little girl is almost two years old, and it breaks my heart that she'll never see the Olympics as they were when I was a kid.

Someday, I'm going to explain to her very clearly just how much I used to love the Olympics. How important I once thought they were. How I tore a medal chart out of a magazine when I was a kid and kept score throughout the Montreal games. How Dorothy Hamill was the first woman I ever loved. How I will always remember Olga Korbut and Nadia Comaneci and Mark Spitz and Bruce Jenner. I need to explain how wonderful and pure the Olympics once seemed.

If I can explain that, she will understand what a tragedy it is to see the games prostituted for the almighty dollar. What a sin it is that marketing and money can deprive us of the miracles only the Olympics can provide.

Especially the one no one will ever forget.

I was twelve years old when the American hockey team stunned the Soviets in Lake Placid. I still remember where I was when I watched it, and I remember even more vividly the following Monday, in the locker room at school, when the chant began.

U-S-A! U-S-A! U-S-A!

From every corner of the room we shouted and pounded on lockers, all of us, just like thousands of other kids across America that day. Only in our case it was different, because most of us weren't American. I was a student at the United Nations International School, where more than half the student body was made up of the children of U.N. diplomats. My classmates came from all over the world: Luyen was from China, Justin from France, Jean-Francis from Canada, Henry from Madagascar; I was from New York. But we chanted together that day and celebrated a win that belonged not to a nation but to everyone who believes in miracles.

That was not just inarguably the greatest moment in sports

history; it was much more. It brought people together in a way that only sports can and now it is gone, never to be relived. Our children will never see anything like it. What a shame.

So here's what I pledge to do: When my little girl turns five years old, I'm going to look up some old friends. I'm going to find Luyen and Justin and all those guys, and see if they have kids, too. And we're all going to sit together with our children and watch a tape of that game. Then maybe the kids will under- stand what the Olympics used to be. And I think it will be fun for me, too. I sure would love to chant with my fellow Americans one more time.

•   •   •

I went to see Dr. Gray today, and told her I've been feeling small.

"In what way do you feel small?" she asked.

That's the trouble. If I knew, I wouldn't be here.

"I think it has something to do with the Olympics," I said.

"Tell me."

"Well, I was thinking about the Olympics last night while my daughter was watching *Sesame Street*. There was this song where the animals sing about how they are all the same, despite their differ- ences. It's called 'We Are All Earthlings.' And it got me to thinking, maybe we'd be better off if *we* looked at it that way instead of trying to win more medals than the Germans and Chinese."

"What do you mean?"

"I mean, in a world with all the crap we have going on," I said, "haven't we outgrown holding sporting competitions against other nations? It seems to me, if we are fighting one country in a war, it's bad form to be playing another in water polo."

"Isn't this really more about your daughter than the Olympics, Michael?"

I just smiled. *If I knew that, I wouldn't be here.*

I felt a familiar need to change the subject, so I tried out a riff I had in mind for the show about the old woman I saw out of context today. She was crossing the street outside Starbucks. I knew her from somewhere but I couldn't place it. It bothered me the whole day, until it finally hit me that it was the woman from Dunkin' Donuts. Every morning at four o'clock I stop at the Dunkin' Donuts for my coffee, and every morning—for six years now—there is an older woman, probably in her late seventies, sitting alone in the corner, surrounded by textbooks. In all these years, I have never spoken to her, never offered even a casual wave. Who is she? I never wondered until I saw her today, out of context. Now I am dying to know her story.

Dr. Gray was unimpressed. "What is it you came to talk about today, Michael?"

"I don't know."

I made a mental note to scrap the Dunkin' Donuts idea. That story sucked. And I could tell Dr. Gray was frustrated, so I tried to say something meaningful.

"Sometimes I think I could have ten great things going on in my life, but my mind always manages to fixate on the one thing I'm worried about."

"You, Michael, may have a syndrome we call the Eleventh Thing."

Why do I have these conversations? Now I didn't feel like talking at all, so I sat in silence until she finally tapped me on the shoulder.

"Hey," she said, "what do you think it is that makes you feel small?"

Come on, Doc. If I knew that, I wouldn't be writing this.

An hour later

Okay, it's an hour later. Forgive me for writing so soon, but I just got into bed and was about to fall asleep when I suddenly sprang bolt upright. For me, this is highly unusual—as it would be for anyone whose alarm clock is set for 3:45 A.M. And I am certainly not one of those people who get brilliant ideas in the middle of the night—hell, the next brilliant idea that comes to me at any time of day may be the first. But tonight I may actually have figured something out.

You see, I made two phone calls just before I got into bed. The first was to my wife, who was working late in her office. I will now do my best to re-create that call from memory.

ME: I'll tell you, honey, I'm really struggling with my therapy. Sometimes I feel it is a complete waste of my time. I don't think it's getting me anywhere. Half the time I find myself going off on pointless tangents just to see if I think they'll work on the radio. The efforts to delve deeply into my psyche are going nowhere, and that frustrates me. I think she's trying, and I think she's competent, but I don't feel like it's going anywhere and I'm thinking of giving it up.

HER *(long pause, during which I can hear that she is typing. Then, finally . . .):* I'm sorry, honey, that sounds like a tough day. Can I ask you something? Why do they call blond kids "towheads"? Paige, from my office, referred to her son as a towhead, and I had to Google it to find out what she meant. I was afraid she was telling me something was wrong with him. I actually think I may have told her how sorry I was about it; she must think I'm a lunatic. But, seriously, why do they use that expression, do you know?

ME: I'm really not sure, honey. I'm going to sleep. See you tomorrow.

Not feeling sated, I then called my dad. I would never get into my feelings about therapy with him, but I thought maybe we could talk a little about life. After all, he'd been a busy lawyer with two kids; he could probably relate to the feelings I was having.

ME: I'll tell you, Dad, sometimes it just seems like it's too much. I work so hard, and so many hours, with all the travel and all the commitments, and then any free time I have I feel obligated to spend with the baby. And it isn't that I don't love her or love being with her, but I haven't seen a movie in two years. I'm not even talking about in a theater—I haven't had time to sit on the couch and watch a movie since she was born. In fact, if it wasn't my job, I probably wouldn't have seen a ball game, either. Anything I do just for myself makes me feel guilty. Like if I'm sneaking in nine quick holes of golf, I can't escape the feeling that I should be spending time with the baby. And that ends up ruining whatever fun the experience might be anyway. Did you ever feel that way when I was a little kid?

HIM (*even longer pause than hers, but without the typing*): Sounds like a tough day, Michael. I'm sorry to hear it. Let me ask you something, while I have you on the phone. What is a country song by someone named "Cyrus"? Fifteen letters. I think it starts with an *A*.

ME: "Achy Breaky Heart."

HIM: What's that?

ME: A-c-h-y B-r-e-a-k-y. Heart.

HIM: It fits.

ME: It's right, Dad, trust me. I'm going to sleep.

And I did just that. Until I sat up so fast it hurt my neck. Because I think I have figured out the reason I go see Dr. Gray every week, even when I don't believe it's doing me any good. I think it is because she's the only person who really listens to me. That's funny, because millions of people hear me talk every day. But sometimes I think Dr. Gray is the only one who really listens. I can't decide if that's a good reason or a bad reason to be seeing her. Or if it means I should stop going or I should never, ever stop. But it seemed worth writing down. Now, if you'll excuse me, I really need to get some sleep.

•   •   •

Funny to read that last part again as I sit down to write tonight, because just now I am thinking I'm actually better off when no one listens to me. Certainly I would have had an easier time this week if my wife had spent it not listening to me rather than not speaking to me.

This fight may have been my fault, though. Or maybe it was both our faults. Or, hell, maybe we just can't help having fights like these. Maybe no one can. And I think I know why.

It's because of the planets.

I've been thinking a lot about that book lately. You remember: the one that said the differences between the sexes are inevitable because men are from Mars and women are from Venus. My wife made me read that book once, and at the time I thought it was drivel. But now, after ten years of marriage, I must say the concept is beginning to make sense. I can think of no more plausible explanation for her behavior than her being from another planet. And I'm sure she feels the same about me.

What I remember best about that book was it said that a woman wants only to be comforted when she is upset. That's *all* she wants. The book said men screw that up because when women come to us with problems, we try to solve them. (Of course we do. Why would you tell someone about a problem if you didn't want them to help solve it?) That's an illustration of the fundamental difference between the sexes. On Mars we solve problems; on Venus they talk about them. According to the book, the only thing my wife wants when she complains is for me to say, "I'm sorry, honey, that really sucks."

Lately, I think I have seen more and more evidence of life from another planet. Sometimes in big, obvious ways. Other times in tiny, insignificant ways. Like underwear. I cannot believe how much time my wife spends talking to other women about underwear. They talk about the benefits of thongs, or the new bra one of them just got, or the right camisole to wear under a sheer blouse; they never stop discussing these garments that no one but their husbands are supposed to see. But, ironically, they *never* discuss them with their husbands.

That's a small thing, but it's important because it's an example of planetary disconnect. So are towels. I could easily spend the rest of my life with just one towel. My wife goes through four a day. I don't have any idea what she does with them all. About the only thing I know is that she has the uniquely feminine ability to wrap a towel about her frame and have it stay in place forever. It's amazing how women are able to do that. If I wrap a towel about my waist it is on the floor within five steps, but even the most flat-chested woman could do aerobics in a towel and it wouldn't budge.

Those are the little differences. But the planetary discord exists on far greater levels, too. It manifests itself in areas much more important than towels and underwear.

For example, if I really am from Mars and she really is from Venus, I'm convinced they don't have sports on Venus. And I don't say that as a sportscaster, just as a guy. The whole notion of the importance of sports is completely lost on my wife. And I don't mean that in any esoteric way; it's very tangible. You see, I firmly believe that football tickets are an acceptable reason for missing a wedding, up to and including first cousins. (Siblings are a different story, though I also believe any sibling should know better than to get married during a Jets game. Funerals are dicey, but Bar Mitzvahs are a slam dunk; I think football tickets are an acceptable excuse for missing any Bar Mitzvah, including your own.)

My wife thinks this is all ludicrous. One time she actually said to me: "They have another game next week, just go to that one." See what I mean? Venusians just don't get it. They don't understand that sports are unlike other forms of entertainment. They don't realize that every football game is a once-in-a-lifetime event: Once you miss it, you've missed it.

This difference of opinion was responsible for World War III in my house this week, because my wife's cousin got married again this morning—a Sunday morning—in Philadelphia.

Here's how it went down:

On Wednesday, out of nowhere, my wife asked me, "What time do we need to leave to make it to Philadelphia by ten?"

So I said, "Why the fuck do we need to be in Philadelphia by ten?"

That was my first mistake. Leading with *fuck* is always a mistake.

"It's Sheila's wedding," she said.

"Who the fuck is Sheila?"

Two mistakes. The first was going with *fuck* again. The second was forgetting the name of a relative. In fact, *you* may even remember this cousin: The first time she got married my wife had to wear green shoes. I should point out, though, in my own defense, that lately this cousin likes to be called Jasmine, and has not been referred to by her regular name in years. She has also been married another time since the green shoes, and has two kids and is still only twenty-eight years old.

"You know perfectly well who Sheila is," my wife said, "and you know that she's getting married Sunday morning."

That's when panic set in.

"What the fuck do you mean Sunday morning?" I asked. "The Jets are playing Sunday."

That was the last *fuck* I was going to be allowed. We have a three-fucks-and-you're-out policy.

"I do not want to discuss this any further," she said. "We are going to the wedding and that's all there is to it."

Now I really regretted the way I had played this thing. If only I could turn back the clock, I think I could have salvaged the situation. In that way, marriage is a lot like putting in golf; it's much easier to judge the break after you've hit it six feet past. What I needed was a marriage mulligan, but I didn't see one being offered.

"How can you even think of missing the most important day of my cousin's life?"

"How exactly have we determined this is the most important day of her life? The woman gets married every other year. She's going to have to take the last name of Gabor by the time she's thirty."

"Now, that's just not fair. I don't give you a hard time about any of your family functions."

"I have no family functions," I said. "My entire family consists of six people."

"Well, whose fault is that?"

I hate when she does that. She throws a non sequitur into the middle of an argument; then, while I'm struggling to recover, she makes a closing remark and leaves the room.

"Just be ready to go by seven," she said, and slammed the door behind her.

Looking back, that really is the topper. She began the whole thing by asking what time we needed to leave, when she obviously knew all along.

So, there I was, on my way to Philadelphia. The worst place to have to go from New York, by the way, because it's not far enough to justify flying but by the time you drive down the New Jersey Turnpike you feel like you've flown to Sydney.

The part I found most confounding was that the Jets were playing the Philadelphia Eagles. *Everyone* at the wedding was going to be wishing they were at the game. We would all be crowded around the little battery-operated television the bartender invariably has, cheering and groaning in unison while the happy couple is cutting the cake. Is that what Sheila wanted? To share her special day with Donovan McNabb and Chad Pennington?

Frankly, I don't understand people who choose to marry during major sporting events. Like people who get married on the Saturday night of the Final Four. Even if they aren't sports fans, they must realize other people are. What they are really saying is: I know I could have picked any other day for this but I don't care; I want half the men at my reception distracted and annoyed.

If you think about it, it is a slap in the face.

Or maybe it's a cost thing. They probably offer huge discounts if you choose these horrendous dates, like Super Bowl Sunday. Who would get married on Super Bowl Sunday? I can't imagine they even offer weddings on that date.

Anyway.

The first thing I found out when I got there was that the bride's father was leaving right after the ceremony. He had tickets to the game. "I figure if I'm out of here by eleven," he told me, "I've got a pretty good shot to make it for kickoff."

"You've got to be kidding," I said. "How did you pull this off?"

"I told her if it was her first marriage, it would have been a different story," he said. "But this is the third wedding at about fifty grand a pop. I told her she had two choices: Either I'm going to see the Eagles, or she could elope."

I grabbed a cocktail napkin. "Do you have a pen?" I asked. "I'd really like to write that down."

"You're coming with me, of course," he said.

"Actually, I wasn't planning to."

"That's bullshit," he said. "You need to see this game."

"Tell that to my wife."

"I will."

Sure enough, two hours later I was on my way to the game. My wife told me that if I had offered to attend the ceremony and skip the reception it would have been fine all along. It frightens me how much I still have to learn about this relationship.

Anyway, I just got home from the game. I must say, the uncle and I had a terrific time. He's a very smart and interesting man. And the Jets won, in overtime. Which means the football game probably lasted longer than the marriage will.

•　　•　　•

I went to see Dr. Gray again this morning, and told her my wife and I have been arguing a lot lately, more than we ever have before. I don't like it. With all the crap going on in my life, this is about the last thing I need.

She told me it's common for couples in our situation—busy professionals with young children—to feel neglected by each other.

"So, what should we do about it?" I asked.

"*Understand* each other," she said.

If that doesn't take the cake; I don't think I would understand my wife if she came with a translator.

"How exactly do we go about doing that?" I asked.

"That challenge has been facing couples since the beginning of time."

I felt an overwhelming need to change the subject. Either that, or kick her in the shin.

"I'm not sleeping so well lately," I said.

"Why is that?"

"Well, my daughter usually wakes me up at some point during the night, which isn't so bad because I used to fall right back to sleep. But the last few weeks, I haven't been. I just lie in bed, thinking."

"Are you thinking about your daughter or your wife?"

"That's the trouble. Sometimes it isn't about my daughter *or* my wife. Actually, I'm thinking about Tom Sawyer."

"Tell me."

"I remember reading that back when I was a kid. The part where they say that work is something you *have* to do, and play is something you *want* to do. Well, I always thought I would find a job that I *wanted* to do so it would never seem like work. And until lately, I thought I had."

"Didn't you use that analogy once before, Michael?" she asked. "I believe it was when you were trying to get your wife pregnant."

"That's right, I did. And this is very much like that. When sex started to feel like work, it really depressed me. And now I feel the same way about my job."

"But a job is supposed to be work."

She wasn't getting it. It isn't my *job* that feels like work. It's *sports*. Being a sports fan is starting to feel like work. It used to be something I wanted to do, but lately it feels more like something I have to do.

"Tell me more, Michael."

I didn't feel like telling her more. She wasn't going to understand, no matter how I tried to explain. I decided to try out a bit for the radio show instead.

"Well, Doc, last night I was thinking about how if I ever watch one episode of a sitcom and then come across the same show a few weeks later, it is *always* the same episode. It has happened too many times to be a coincidence; it is now a phenomenon."

"Michael," Dr. Gray said, "sometimes we force ourselves to become bogged down in the minutiae in order to avoid the real issues in our lives."

"I know that," I told her, "but I don't see what it has to do with this."

"You don't?"

"I don't," I said. "But I *have* noticed that if you have enough channels, the movie *Saturday Night Fever* is always on."

"Do you like that movie?"

"That's the trouble. Sometimes it isn't about whether you like the movie or not, just that it's on."

"If your life was a movie," she asked, "would it be a comedy or a tragedy?"

"Well, comedies always have happy endings and tragedies end with everybody dying. Which one sounds more like life to you?"

"Don't you find happiness in anything?" she asked.

"Like what?"

"How about the beauty of the season?"

"Of course not," I said. "It's autumn."

No fatalist loves autumn. It is a season reserved for optimists. I once heard a guy say he loves winter; boy, did that take me aback.

"Perhaps your melancholy is in part due to the weather," she said.

"I don't know. I hate to think I could be one of those people who become melancholy because of the weather."

Then, just as I was thinking this little routine had potential, Dr. Gray leaned forward in her chair. Her nose was closer to mine than it has ever been. "Michael," she said, "how do you expect your wife to understand you if you don't even understand yourself?"

I didn't say anything to that. In fact, I didn't say anything at all for the rest of the hour. But I have to admit, it was one hell of a good question.

●　　●　　●

I've reached one important conclusion this week, and that is that you aren't really married until you've heard the phrase:

"I'm fat and I hate my clothes."

Tell me, what the hell is a suitable response to that? It is the conundrum husbands have faced since the beginning of time—trying to answer the unanswerable. There is no direction you can go that will not lead you directly into harm's way. If you say, "No, you are not fat," she will invariably say, "Am I as thin as I used to be?" Then you're dead. Because if you say yes you are blatantly lying, and she'll either call you on it or accuse you of paying so little attention that you don't even notice the obvious weight she has gained. So then you'll have to say, "Well, maybe you've gained a little weight," in which case you're dead, because she'll say, "You think I'm fat, don't you?" And you're right back where you started.

I consider "I'm fat and I hate my clothes" to be the seminal sentence of married life. And it reared its ugly head again today, capping what has been a pretty rough month in my house.

But the news is good.

The news is that I've spent enough time thinking about it that I believe I finally have it solved. After Dr. Gray told me I needed to figure *myself* out, it occurred to me that if I can't do that, how can I possibly expect to figure out anyone else? So this morning, when she said, "I'm fat and I hate my clothes," I tried something new.

I punted.

"Honey," I simply said, "there's no good way for me to respond to that."

You see, I've realized that the only answer is just to acknowledge defeat. Stop trying to fight it. Stop trying to say anything at a time when even silence may not save you. There *is* no answer, boys, and the sooner we make peace with that, the sooner we may actually find peace. The answer is to punt, even if you think it's still first down. See if your defense can win it for you.

So I was feeling good, thinking I was going to be able to silently withstand this attack, when she dropped an entirely different bomb on me, one for which I was completely unprepared.

"I'm fat, I'm old, and I'm ugly," she said.

(Now, I know what you're thinking: Not so bad. All I had to say was that she was not fat or old or ugly. The trouble is, she was working two steps ahead of me.)

"You are not fat or old or ugly," I said.

"Which am I the least?"

These conversations are like games of chess, and my wife against me is like Bobby Fischer against Jessica Simpson.

But again, in keeping with my new philosophy, I decided not to fight it. Rather than say anything at all, I resolved to do the following when my wife makes a remark that involves her appearance.

1. I will pretend I didn't hear it. If she says it again I will

2. Excuse myself and leave the room. If she still remembers when I return then

3. It's time for a business trip.

Or, in the case of today, a trip to the supermarket.

Now, I don't know if I've mentioned it, but I hate the supermarket. I detest everything about the experience and, consequently, I seldom go. But today, when my wife hit me with an unanswerable question, the only way I could think to get out was to offer to do the food shopping.

Unfortunately, I cannot spend more than three minutes in the supermarket without calling her, so it sort of defeats the purpose. In fact, I have no idea how men ever did the food shopping before cell phones, because I invariably have to use mine at least five times to ask questions.

"Honey, they don't have the Philadelphia cream cheese in the block, they only have it in the tub, unless we want the fat-free. Which do we want?"

That last—"we"—is laughable, isn't it? Obviously, the issue is not which *we* want, but which *she* wants, because if I had so much as a vote in this, I wouldn't have to call every two minutes. Let's face it, she decides which brands we use. I'm not sure when I ceded control of that, but I'd bet it happened right around the time I realized it all *really* mattered to her.

Frankly, I don't know which brand of toilet tissue I used to buy when I was single. In fact, I'm sure there was not one brand I used to buy, just as there was not one brand of tuna fish or deodorant or peanut butter. The things I was passionate about then are the same few that I still am today: Kellogg's cornflakes, Tropicana orange juice, Dannon yogurt. Otherwise, when I ask, "Which brand do we buy?" what I am really saying is "Which brand do you like?" Because we both know I don't give a shit. I cannot for the life of me tell all these different brands of cottage cheese apart; they are less different than the identical black shoes in my wife's closet.

So as I walked the aisles this afternoon, I found myself wondering just how women became so specific. (This was right after I called to ask whether the butter we use is salted or unsalted.) I was pushing my overflowing cart down the produce aisle, watching some woman demonstrate for her husband the proper way to squeeze a melon, when, just like that, it all became clear to me. Suddenly, I understood the dynamic that dictates my relationship with my wife, and the thread of commonality I have with all men everywhere. And it is so bloody simple I can't believe it took me this long to figure it out.

We are all married to women who think we are idiots.

It's that simple. Your wife thinks you are an idiot and mine thinks the same of me. In fact, my wife also thinks *you* are an idiot. But don't take that personally: It's a gender thing; all women think all men are idiots.

This crosses all boundaries, including race, religion, and socioeconomic status. Rich guys and poor, black ones and white, Christians and Jews and Muslims—every man everywhere has a wife who thinks he just doesn't get it. This has nothing to do with intelligence, book smarts, street smarts, or any of the other traditional means of measuring brains; the simple reality is that men and women are operating on different wavelengths and that disconnect makes it inevitable that a woman will someday look upon her husband and think: I just have no idea what goes on in your head.

Now, the questions: Why doesn't that disconnect work both ways? Why don't men become frustrated when their wives don't get it?

The answer: Because men don't care.

Mostly, we just want to be left alone. And a woman's need to discuss our problems only interferes with our need to pretend they do not exist. This is the central difference between a husband and a wife.

We men do not believe our wives are idiots, because we take them at face value; they are what they are. Women, meanwhile, see us for what they think we *could* be, or *should* be. (Marlon Brando described it in *Guys and Dolls* as cutting men up into different shapes and sizes, depending upon how they're wearing husbands this year.) Women do that; yours does, mine does, they all do. And we resist it, and that's what makes us idiots.

This goes for all men, even the smartest and most successful. I guarantee you George Will's wife calls her girlfriends the moment her husband leaves the house in the morning and says, "You're not going to believe what that schmuck did last night." Now, what George probably did was finish some correspondence with several heads of state, write a column for *Newsweek*, and calculate the combined batting average of the Chicago Cubs dating back to the last time they won the World Series. But maybe his bow tie didn't match his socks while he did it, so now she is making fun of his different shades of brown while he is on his way to the White House for an exclusive interview with the secretary of defense.

How about the Boss, George Steinbrenner? One of the most influential and powerful men in the nation, he makes millionaire ballplayers with guaranteed contracts tremble. But don't think for one minute he doesn't return home after negotiating a billion-dollar deal and step out of his limousine to find his wife waiting in the driveway with her arms folded across her chest and *that* look on her face.

"Now you listen to me, Mister Most Powerful Man in Baseball . . ."

I'll bet the driver gets out of there quickly on those nights; probably because he has the same thing waiting for him at home.

Of course, you must realize that this issue is insurmountable. We certainly aren't going to change, and it isn't fair to expect us to. Men are actually ridiculously easy creatures to understand; women are just trying too hard. Their problem is they cannot conceive of just shutting off their minds. We can. We do it all the time. Women need to stop trying to figure out what we are thinking, because most of the time we are not.

So there I was today in the supermarket, standing by the deli, holding a number that would not be called for half an hour, watching all the other men read notes with very precisely written instructions, when I realized I finally have it all figured out.

It's not about understanding *them*. It's about understanding *ourselves*. If our wives want to believe we're idiots, let them. From now on, that's going to be just fine with me. I have neither the desire nor the energy to fight any longer. I know that she loves me, and anything beyond that doesn't have to matter.

Besides, what are the options? We can either try to live *without* them—good luck with that—or try to live *with* them, which is what I pledge to do. And if that means accepting the fact that she thinks I'm an idiot, I can do it. And I will—from this day forward—be at peace with it. And all I ask is one thing in return: Every now and again, I would like just a few minutes of uninterrupted quiet to watch the ball game.

THIRD TRIP
to the Supermarket

October 2003 – January 2004

Disillusionment

If I seem cranky this morning, I suppose it is because I am.

I'm sorry; I guess we don't always approach every day with the reverence it deserves. Today I feel particularly bogged down in the minutiae. And, also, I am sucking my thumb.

Now, I could leave that without explanation and make you spend the rest of the day wondering why the hell Greeny was sucking his thumb. But my inclination is to think that might just be more aggravating than intriguing. So to be on the safe side I am going to explain it, but I want it on record that it might have been funnier left to the imagination.

Right now my left thumb is on injured reserve.

Dress-shirt accident.

Who was it that came up with the idea of placing tiny pins inside dress shirts, anyway? Wouldn't you like five minutes alone with that guy? What purpose do the pins serve? The shirt is already neatly folded and tightly packaged in cellophane—what are the pins for? And why are there so many of them? You can never find them all, there's always one hiding that scares the hell out of you when you're putting the shirt on, and after that you have to watch your step for the rest of the day because one of them invariably falls and becomes lost in the carpeting, which is particularly frightening with my kids running around. It's a lot like the land-mine problem.

I guess I should tell you there is another reason I am cranky, and that is because yesterday my wife informed me that we have to go pick out stationery for the children. She even went so far as to say the kids are "well overdue" for letterhead of their own.

Now, I'm not sure what correspondence it is she thinks they are having, but I tried very hard to explain to her that since one of them cannot write yet and the other cannot even talk yet, it seems ridiculous to buy them personalized stationery. I also told her I was afraid that the purchase would lead to the advancement of my greatest pet peeve.

Notes written in the first person from babies.

You know what I mean:

Dear Uncle Phil,

Thank you so much for the Thomas the Tank Engine play set and matching accessories. My brother and I play with them every day and sometimes fight over who gets to be the engineer. My mommy says you must come see me play with it all because it is so cute. Hope to see you before I turn three.

Love,
Joshua

I am proud to say that neither of my children has ever written a first-person letter. That's one area where I've put my foot down and it hasn't been stomped on by my wife. But I fear the purchase of this stationery could be a dangerous step in that direction.

I am almost tempted to call my wife's father. If he caught wind of this, he'd help me set her straight. He is a product of a different era, a time when parents didn't need personalized stationery for their children. For that matter, they somehow managed to raise children without microwaves, disposable diapers, or Mr. Bubble. I know *we* could never survive without those.

But the issue here is stationery, and the fact that my life has become an endless stream of gifts and thank-you notes. Has this happened to you, too? For me it happened overnight, or at some other time when I wasn't paying attention. All of a sudden, my daily routine always includes stopping at Tiffany or Petit Bateau to buy a crystal vase or a onesie-and-matching-nightcap. And I am suddenly obligated to handwrite a note to every friend generous enough to invite us for a drink. In fact, I think we have reached a point where the thank-you is more important than the gift itself.

What someone needs to do—and to whomever is brave enough I pledge five hundred dollars—is put a stop to this cycle. Let us all unanimously agree that when someone performs an act of kindness, we appreciate it. That way, every time we send a gift or host a dinner party, we can just assume our generosity was noted and valued and then we can get on with our lives.

Think of the time and energy we could save.

Now, you may be wondering what the hell this has to do with sports. And the obvious answer is: not a thing. But maybe that's the whole point. Maybe sometimes, it isn't about sports. Sometimes it's just about how hard it is to write a thank-you note on an infant's personal stationery while you are sucking your thumb.

●　●　●

Well, I'm back.

Eleven months after the mushroom cloud that is my son dropped into my life, a familiar angst has crept back into my soul. And so I have reluctantly opened this journal again, in hopes of quieting my aching mind.

That's the major problem: I just can't find anywhere quiet to go. Perhaps here, alone with my thoughts, I can find five quiet minutes. At this point, I honestly believe I would pay any amount of money for that. Just for five quiet minutes. Maybe not *any* amount; let's say twenty thousand dollars. I feel I can safely say I would pay twenty grand for five minutes of total silence.

This has been going on for a while, since right around the day my son came home from the hospital. I believe I held out this long without writing for two reasons. The first is: I just wanted to believe I was beyond it. I thought after coming to terms with my wife, I had solved the greatest riddle known to mankind. I thought I would coast from there well into middle age at least. But then my little boy came along and the ruckus began. Now there is *no* time when one of them isn't awake, when one of them isn't around, when someone doesn't need something from me. (The notion that being *needed* is essential to the human experience, by the way, is the greatest load of crap since New Coke. I would give another twenty grand just to spend a full day without anyone needing me for anything. Last month I got strep throat and my wife quarantined me to the guest room; it was the best weekend of my life. No one expected anything of me. That's what I've sunk to. I'm nostalgic about a Group A streptococcus infection.)

The other reason I waited so long to start writing is because I convinced myself that the chaos was temporary. Actually, my daughter convinced me of that. She lulled me into a false sense of security. When *she* first came home everything was up for grabs, but it wasn't long before we stabilized. And got into a routine. And soon enough, I was all right. I keep waiting for that to happen again. I am still waiting. I'll let you know if it ever does.

The way I see it is this: The first child is like having a hurricane blow through your life. At first it's a mess, but then you pick yourself up, straighten the furniture, and reclaim some degree of normalcy. The second is like an atom bomb. Any routine you have is tossed right out with the bathwater.

This is especially true, I think, when they are born in the order ours were. Little girls are much easier than little boys. (I am anticipating that to be the case until she discovers boys, by which time I am hoping to be mercifully dead.) My daughter, now almost four years old, was angelic from her first hour and remains indescribably easy; if you give her a book and say, "Wait here," an hour later she'll be right where you left her.

My son is a year old and if you leave *him* alone for an hour you'll find him in Cleveland. People are impressed with his early walking, but in my opinion it is a curse. The ability to walk is not something a child should have until he is aware enough to avoid the catastrophes that lie around every corner. There isn't a coffee table in the county my son hasn't crashed into. The child's face looks as though he's gone ten rounds with Mike Tyson.

Now, please don't misunderstand: I love him every bit as much as I love her, and I couldn't possibly love anything more than I love them both. But these are not easy times. So, reluctantly, I have opened this journal again, with two different hopes. The first is that I can make some sense of the way I am feeling. The second is that I can share some of what I believe I have learned.

This week, in particular, has been a greater education than I received in four years of college. I implore you to learn from it, from my mistakes, my suffering.

Here's the situation: *My wife left me.*

How about that for drama? If this were my radio show I would leave a lengthy pause before the explanation, because the explanation is a whole lot less dramatic. The explanation is: She had a work conference in Arizona that lasted the whole week. But, frankly, she might as well have run off with a pharmacist for all the help she was around the house.

So for five days I was completely alone with the two children. (Actually, the live-in nanny was there, but the net loss was one adult. There was just me and Lourdes with the kids, which means we no longer had them outnumbered; we could still go to a zone defense if we wanted, but we couldn't double-cover either of them. And that spells trouble; you have a better chance of shutting down Shaquille O'Neal by yourself than you do my son.)

Through the misery and the mess, I arrived at five simple rules every parent should understand—particularly dads who might otherwise have no idea.

1. If you find a minivan you cannot identify in your driveway, run.

I arrived home to find that Lourdes had organized a play date. Seems this goes on at my house every Monday. Who knew? I walked in to discover nine four-year-olds running amok in my family room, all of them eating peanut butter. (There is no messier substance on earth than peanut butter; it is the Silly Putty of food. Children play with it every bit as much as they eat it. In fact, my daughter was playing with it when I came home; her game seemed to consist solely of smearing peanut butter on every slice of bread in the house. I don't know that she ate any of them.) I stood it as long as I could, but after about ninety seconds I pulled Lourdes aside and whispered in her ear, "I'm going upstairs. When all these children are gone, please come get me. You'll find me under the bed in a fetal position."

2. You cannot remove snot from cashmere.

This is another one I found out the hard way, when I made the incalculably bad decision to wear a John Varvatos turtleneck despite my son's case of the sniffles. That lasted about five minutes before I found a round smear of wet snot just below the left shoulder. I did not panic at first, which turned out to be a mistake; I would have been better off panicking than trying to wipe away the snot with a tissue. Before I knew it, I had created a disgusting work of art. The tiny flecks of tissue became embedded in the fabric and the snot did not disappear, it only became less wet. But even then I did not panic; I just took the sweater off and held it under the kitchen faucet. Soon I had turned a six-hundred-dollar sweater into papier-mâché. Each day since, I have changed clothes in the car before entering the house. I recommend cotton sweatshirts; any damage a runny nose can do is only temporary.

3. You cannot vacuum puke off a tile floor.

This began after I made the mistake of insisting that my daughter try the macaroni and cheese. I even found myself speaking those fourteen words I swore I never would.

"How do you know you don't like it if you've never even tried it?"

She threw it up on the kitchen floor. I guess that was how she knew.

Either way, I was left to my own devices on this one because it was Wednesday, the one night of the week when Lourdes goes to church. In fairness to Lourdes, she had already done everything for this dinner short of eating it herself—which, in retrospect, I wish she'd done too. If she'd thrown it up, at least she would probably have made it to the bathroom in time.

My daughter did not. She made it to about two feet from the dishwasher. So now I had to get her quieted down and rebathed (I believe vomiting requires a rebathing; call me old-fashioned), then get both kids into bed before I could tend to the mess on the kitchen floor.

I will confess that before I began cleaning, I pulled out the yellow pages and begged several cleaning crews to come out. But it was after eight o'clock, so no one was open and mostly I was begging answering services. Next I gave some thought to leaving the mess for Lourdes, but it occurred to me that if someone did that to me I would quit on the spot, and if she quit and left me alone with the children I would have driven into the path of an oncoming truck before Friday.

There was no choice but to attack this problem myself.

I found rubber gloves beneath the sink and wrapped a thick necktie around my nose, then bent to inspect the evidence. What I found was a substance more solid than I had expected. It looked as though it could almost be swept up with a broom. I was, in fact, going for the broom when I came across the vacuum cleaner. It seemed to me that if the broom was going to work, why not the vacuum? I opted to give it a shot.

Let me ask a question: Have you ever seen the way vomit congeals when exposed to a burst of air? It is a sight to behold. So now I am down one vacuum cleaner, which I will have to replace before the housekeeper misses it.

Worse, I had an even more grotesque mess on the kitchen floor. So what I did was retrieve the entire Sunday *New York Times* from the recycling bin and use that to mop up. By the time I got through "Arts and Leisure" there was almost no sign of any puke left, but there was a horrid gray reflection in the tile, the same color your hands turn after an hour with the newspaper. I decided *that* could be left for Lourdes, which it was, along with a note that read: "I didn't know which cleaner to use for the kitchen floor. The kids did not like the macaroni and cheese."

4. When alone with the children, hide the key to the liquor cabinet.

Hide it from *yourself.* And not because you will be inclined to drink while caring for them—I actually recommend that—but because there will come that one moment when the baseball game is starting and the baby is crying and you will begin to eye the sippy cup and the Johnnie Walker Black at the same time.

How much could it possibly take? A shot? A thimbleful? And how much harm could it *really* do? Permanent damage? Stunting of growth? Predisposition to alcoholism? Do we really believe a quarter sip of Scotch could wreak *that* much havoc? And think of the good it could do—the peace, the quiet, the baseball you could watch unmolested if the children were busy sleeping one off.

Ultimately, if you are like me, you won't do it because the last thing you need is for your wife to come home and find the toddler in a twelve-step program. But do yourself a favor and avoid the temptation—remove the option, and be sure you do it before the first pitch is thrown.

5. Never bring home one of anything.

This began so innocently. I was walking past a toy store with no intention of buying anything when a large Clifford the Big Red Dog caught my eye. My daughter has always loved Clifford, and has a room filled with stuffed Cliffords, as well as all the other dogs on his show. (And yes, I know their names are T-Bone, Cleo, and Mac.)

Just the night before, my son had watched a Clifford video for the first time and seemed to really like it, so it occurred to me that he would probably like to have a stuffed doggie, too, just like his big sister. I went in and actually asked, "How much is that doggie in the window?" (The heavily pierced salesgirl didn't bat an eye at that, by the way. She didn't even know which dog was Clifford. I had to explain that he was the big red one, hence the name Clifford the Big Red Dog.)

When I'd finally schlepped the giant animal home, I was ecstatic to present it. I even went so far as to enlist my daughter to help because I'd decided she would be thrilled to see her little brother getting his first Clifford.

Reading those words now I realize how naïve they are, but at the time I did not see it coming. Not until those big brown eyes watered up and she asked, "Did you get *me* a Clifford, too?"

Uh-oh.

"No, honey, you have so many of them I thought it would be nice if your brother had one, too, because he wants to be just like his big sister."

"You got my brother a new Clifford and you didn't get me anything?"

When she put it that way, it sounded so different from how it had sounded in my head. I wanted to explain that to her. I wanted to tell her that Daddy just wasn't thinking at the time, that Daddy is in his busiest season and ratings are announced next week and the pressure is so heavy sometimes he thinks he might suffocate, and to top it off Mommy is gone all friggin' week. But she's four, so none of that would mean anything to her.

"Honey," I said, struggling, "you have so many Cliffords already."

"Not like this one."

"Sweetheart, they're all the same."

"No they're not," she said. "This one has ears and a bone in his mouth."

She reminds me more of her mother every day.

Well, both children are asleep now, with a new Clifford in his crib and her room covered in all the stickers I had to let her put up to quiet her tears. I will have a tough time explaining those to the wife when she gets back. And she is due any minute, but that's all right, even if she gets a little angry. I'm looking forward to seeing her anyway.

•   •   •

I went to see Dr. Gray today. It had been a while, more than a year. I told her I was writing again. I told her the combination of two kids and one very busy job had me right on the edge of losing my patience.

She told me my feelings were very common.

Then she stopped.

I guess she was waiting for me to say something, but, really, what the hell was there to say to that? Was I supposed to thank her for telling me that my issues were not unique? I can't decide if that makes me feel better or worse. Perhaps it would be nice to have a truly distinctive set of neuroses. That way, if I'm going to be unhappy, at least I can feel I'm accomplishing something.

When I did speak again, I found myself talking about something entirely different.

"What I have come to believe, Doc," I said, "is that there is nothing in the world better than low expectations."

"What does that have to do with what we were talking about, Michael?" she asked.

Isn't it her job to figure that out? It's bad enough that this crap pops into my head—can't someone else figure out where it's coming from? It's all I can do to deal with it while it's here.

"Tell me about expectations," she said.

"Well," I said, "it seems to me that, on some level, life is all about your expectations. For example, the whole idea of a glass being half empty or half full. I think the world has that analogy backward. The person with great expectations, which are a curse, sees a glass as *only* half full. While someone with more modest expectations says the glass is *only* half empty. It's still about the way you view the glass, but everyone assumes 'half full' is the more desirable option. It strikes me that the guy who is *satisfied* with half a glass is going to be much happier."

"Do you think you are on the side of half full or half empty?" she asked.

"I think I've got, like, a sip left."

"So I suppose the trick is to feel satisfied with that sip."

"I suppose it is," I said. "But how do you do that?"

"That's exactly what we're trying to figure out."

Essentially, she was telling me that the key to happiness is to be happy, and when I asked how to do it she admitted she hadn't a fucking clue. So why am I sitting here?

"Let me ask you this," she said, as I was getting up to leave. "Is there anything that makes you happy? I mean *really* happy. Is there anything that makes you happy every time you think of it?"

"I don't know."

"Think about it," she said.

So I'm thinking about it.

Only one thing has come to mind so far, and that is the story of how my son was born. It was an unusual birth, even though there was nothing at all unusual about the delivery; it was only unusual because the birth announcement was made by a plumber.

I'll tell you about that in a minute, but in order for you to understand it I must first explain that my wife has really never been impressed with me. That's one of the things I've come to terms with. I mean *really* never, going all the way back to our first date. The day we affectionately refer to as when we "fed the rich."

It was in Chicago, where we both lived, and we'd been introduced and had chatted a bit and I decided to ask her to a charity event, a Thanksgiving program, where local celebrities would deliver dinners to needy families. I invited her because I thought it would make me look philanthropic, and because I thought anything that attached the word *celebrity* to my name seemed like a chick magnet. (Plus it was a good cause.)

So, the day before Thanksgiving we loaded up my car. We got turkey, stuffing, mashed potatoes, gravy, cranberry sauce, green beans, corn bread, pumpkin pie, and an address in a sketchy part of town. I remember it all like it's happening now. She wore a chocolate-brown cashmere turtleneck and the same perfume she still wears today.

Everything was going fine until we arrived at the recipient's apartment building. I was expecting bullet holes and missing windows. I was surprised instead to find a doorman.

"How could anyone who lives in a doorman building need to have Thanksgiving dinner delivered?" I asked.

She didn't say anything. She was too busy looking skeptical.

Once inside, we told the doorman the name of the family we were there to see and he buzzed upstairs, and then we were on our way up in an elevator with clean carpets and a notice on the wall informing the tenants of the date for the holiday party. (For the record, the building I grew up in wasn't demonstrably nicer than this.)

Then we were in the apartment, and while it wasn't lavish, it certainly wasn't awful. There was a full complement of worn but clean furniture and an unseen baby crying loudly, which I interpreted as a sign of poverty. (Shows you what I knew; if that were true, the house I live in now would be condemned.)

"Thank you for coming," the lady of the house said. "It's been a bad week."

"Why is that?" I asked.

"The cable has been out," she said. "My husband will flip if he can't watch his football."

Fabulous.

"Well, I hope you enjoy the dinner," I said. "Happy Thanksgiving."

"Thank you," the lady said. "God bless you."

We didn't say anything until we got to the car but I could see from the look on my wife's face that she was unimpressed. It is a look I have since come to know quite well.

"So what did you think?" I asked.

"It wasn't quite what I expected," she said. "I feel like a caterer."

That was how it began and, frankly, it's been about like that ever since. I can honestly say I have seen my wife really impressed with me only one time in all the years we have been together and that was the day my son was born.

It was a Tuesday morning and when I got off the air the following message was on my voice mail:

"Michael, the septic backed up into the basement again. There is raw sewage in the basement. It actually backed up into the washing machine, so there is raw sewage in the washing machine. I'm freaking out. My new Seven jeans from Henry Lehr were in there, and this can't be good for the baby. You have to get the plumber out here. I'm going to get a pedicure."

When I called, that's where she was, getting a pedicure, calmer after a half hour with her feet in warm water but still upset about the sewage. I managed to get hold of the plumber quickly and was driving home to meet him when my cell phone rang.

"Change in plans," my wife said. "I'm on my way to the hospital."

Her water broke in the pedicurist's chair.

I called my brother and asked him to race to my house and deal with the plumber. (I couldn't allow Lourdes to handle that. She is sweet and wonderful with children but she doesn't speak English and refuses to acknowledge it, so she nods at anything you say. If I left *her* to deal with the problem, I feared I'd come home to find she'd unwittingly agreed to serve as an apprentice to the plumber and would be leaving the next morning.)

Then I was off to the delivery room.

My only experience with this room was with my first child. That was nine hours of labor and fifty minutes of pushing, which was rough for me, and all I was doing was holding a leg and cheering. When I got to the hospital this time and found my wife hooked up to all the equipment, a rush of familiarity washed over me. Then the most important person in the world arrived.

The anesthesiologist.

I think the arrival of the Messiah would have less impact on a pregnant woman than the guy who gives the epidural. My wife looked as excited as the girls in the audience of *The Ed Sullivan Show* the night the Beatles were on.

"Doctor, I'm so happy to see you," she said. "I want the maximum. No, more than the maximum. I don't want to feel anything."

The doctor flashed the knowing smile of one who hears that speech a lot. Then he turned to me and said the last thing I was expecting.

"Hey, you're Greeny! I listen to your show every morning. I'm a big Jets fan."

Before I could say anything, my wife jumped in. "Michael can get you into any Jets game you want. He'll give you a tour of the studio too, if you want one. Would you like to meet Chad Pennington?"

Then she gave *me* a look that said, "If you don't turn on that so-called charm right now, this will be the closest you get me to a bed for the rest of our marriage."

"So, Doc," I said, "you think we'll make the play-offs next year?"

Just then, the doctor got paged. He hadn't even begun placing the needle into the small of my wife's back yet. (That had made me queasy the first time and I had planned to step out of the room for it, but now I feared that my wife might castrate me with the umbilical cord if I tried.) When the doctor went to attend to an emergency, promising to be right back, she grabbed me by the lapels. "You promise this guy anything he wants, do you understand? Tell him he can have *your* season tickets if he wants them."

"I'll do my best."

"Just keep him talking," she told me. "Keep him in the room."

When the doctor returned, I ran through the entire history of the Jets organization with him, year by year, while he prepared the drugs for my wife. When he was done, he actually sat in a chair and chatted with me for a good half hour until a nurse came and insisted she needed him desperately.

"By now you should be feeling a little warm rush," he told my wife, and by the look on her face I could see she did. "I'll come back as soon as I can."

When he was gone I went to her side and she took my hand and squeezed it. There was an expression on her face I didn't recognize. I had never seen it before, nor have I since. But I remember it well.

That's the only thing I can think of that makes me happy all the time, at least the only thing I can think of right now. I must remember to tell Dr. Gray about it next week.

By the way, the conclusion of the story is, my cell phone rang while we were holding hands. It was my brother. The plumber was saying the septic system was completely shot and needed to be replaced.

"Honey, I need to take this call," I said, and drifted away from the bed. "How much will it cost me to replace the entire thing?"

"I don't know," the plumber said.

"How fast can it be done?"

"I don't know that either."

"Well, you're a fountain of information," I said. "Do you think you could find those out for me and call back as soon as you can? I'm in the hospital right now having a baby."

"I'll call you back as fast as I can."

About two hours later I heard the doctor tell my wife: "Here it comes, just give me one more push."

A moment after that, the baby came. And not five seconds later my cell phone rang. I would never have answered except that I wanted running water when this baby came home.

It was the plumber. "Mr. Greenberg, I can probably have the work done for you by the end of the week," he said, "but it's going to cost about twelve grand."

"Just do it," I said. "Fast as you can."

"All right."

"Is my brother still there?" I asked.

"Yeah, and your parents are here, too."

"Great," I said, and watched as the nurse laid my son on his mother's chest for the first time. "Tell them it's a boy."

.   .   .

Well, this seemed like a good idea. But as the saying goes, the best-laid plans of mice and men are frequently screwed up by billionaires. And in the annals of hideous, humiliating social disasters, this one took the cake.

Here's what happened: I was invited to speak at a banquet in Miami Beach, for a group of retired accountants. And since the weather is starting to turn cold, and since we haven't been alone for ten consecutive seconds since the baby was born, my wife decided to come with me. We called it a mini-vacation.

Terrific.

Then it got better: We mentioned our plans to the Billionaires and they jumped on board. Literally. Meaning, they flew us down on their plane. And let me tell you, that didn't suck. In fact, if you've never been on a private plane—there simply is *no* other way to fly.

Forget the lines, forget the hassles, forget the hurry.

Want to know when takeoff is? Whenever the hell you want it to be.

You drive right up to the plane, someone takes your bags, escorts you on board, and the next thing you know you're in a leather recliner that would give Yao Ming enough room to stretch his legs.

The movie? Whatever you want it to be.

The food? Whatever you want it to be.

The lighting? Whatever you want it to be.

Honestly, when the pilot announced we were beginning our approach into Fort Lauderdale, I asked him to keep going. (By the way, the "announcement" was a little different from the norm, too. Essentially, the captain opened the cockpit door, walked over, and said, "We're beginning our approach into Fort Lauderdale.")

All that was fine. Better than fine—it was terrific.

Then we arrived at the hotel, where just about the entire staff recognized me. Now, that recognition is always nice, but when you're checking into a hotel with a guy who just gave you a ride on his jet, the high five from the bellman feels particularly good. So I was in a fine mood to that point, as well. We agreed to meet by the pool in twenty minutes.

My wife and I were wading in the shallow end, basking in the golden rays of a glorious South Florida afternoon, when the Billionaires came walking toward us. I took one look and had absolutely no idea what to do. There was nowhere to run, nowhere to hide. I was trapped in the swimming pool. With Mr. Billionaire headed right toward me. Wearing a Speedo.

I don't know how to begin to describe the horror, the anguish.

It was just *so* wrong.

So.

Completely.

Ridiculous.

I couldn't stop staring. And I'll bet you can guess *where* I was staring. Although it certainly wasn't because there was anything appealing about it. There is no man alive who should wear that bathing suit, least of all a paunchy fifty-six-year-old businessman. (Oh yeah, did I mention he is a generation older than I? While his wife is *seven years younger than I am?* Had I forgotten to mention that? Sorry, perhaps my memory was temporarily shattered by the sight of his onions.)

"Hey there, Greenbergs!" he shouted amiably, oblivious to how mortified I was. "How about a cocktail?"

"Sounds good," I said, in part because I couldn't think of anything else to say, and also because I suddenly had the urge to be the most drunk I have ever been.

"Piña colada sound good?" he asked.

Mind you, he was shouting these questions to me from the pool deck, a good fifty feet away, so not only could everyone *between* us hear him, so could everyone *around* us. It must be that having a billion dollars removes any shred of self-consciousness. Although, even if I could buy and sell Bill Gates five times over, my wife would never allow me to wear that bathing suit. Not even inside the house.

"I don't know," I said. "I'm not a piña colada kind of guy."

"Come on," he said, "have something sweet."

I looked around. I could see the faces of the bell staff, the lifeguards, the waiters, all doing double takes as they alternated staring at me and Mr. Billionaire's package.

"Make mine a Scotch!" I shouted.

My wife gave me a puzzled look.

"Make it a double," I added, "plus a Budweiser on the side!"

You see, I like piña coladas, but I do not like getting caught in the rain. And I absolutely could not bring myself to sip a fruity cocktail next to a guy whose ass was hanging out.

In fact, it was not until I sat beside him and watched him coat his body in sunscreen that I grasped the enormity of what was happening. My mind went into overdrive: *I am going to have to sit here and talk to this guy with a straight face. I can't believe it. He's not South American; he's from freakin' Akron. Where did he even get that thing?* After my double Scotch and beer chaser it was all I could do not to stand on my chair and scream as loudly as I could:

Am I the only one who sees how ridiculous this is?

Then, just when it seemed it could not get worse, it almost did.

While our wives were off swimming—or shopping, or something—a terrific young blonde suddenly appeared at the foot of our chairs, smiling broadly and shielding her eyes from the sun.

"Hey there, you!" she said.

"Ah, baby, you look gorgeous," Mr. Billionaire said, and stood. "How about a big hug?"

Then he's pawing this chick that couldn't have been more than twenty-five years old. They're hugging and she's giggling and I'm frantically scanning the area, looking for a waiter.

"Another Scotch!" I shouted.

"Michael," Mr. Billionaire said, "get up here, I'd like you to meet my daughter."

"Make it a double!" I shouted, to no one in particular. I stood, careful not to brush against the front of Mr. Billionaire's bathing suit. "Pleased to meet you," I said.

She shook my hand. "I've heard so much about you," she said. "You're the one who does the weather on CNN, right?"

"No, honey," her father said. "Michael does the sports show."

"Oh, that's right," she said. "I'm a big fan of yours."

"Thanks," I said, for absolutely no reason.

"So, how's your mother?" he asked her.

I could see the daughter tense up.

"She's fine."

I could read it all in her face now. This had not been an easy divorce.

Dad makes it huge, ditches Mom, marries a girl just a few years older than me, but he sends me money every month so I let him hug me in front of his friends.

I have no idea if any of that is right, but I was drunk so what the hell? It was all I could do not to ask the daughter if she was uncomfortable with her father's genitals.

"Do you live down here?" I asked her.

"Claire is in law school," her father said.

"At the University of Miami," she said. "This is my last year. I'll be coming north soon."

"New York?"

"Tallahassee," she said. "I'm not moving back to the cold. I'm going to clerk for a judge on the state supreme court."

"That's wonderful," I said. "Well, I'll let you two have some time alone. I think I'll take a swim."

I passed the waiter on the way to the pool and took my drink off his tray, shot it down in a single gulp, and replaced the glass. Thankfully, I thought better of swimming—perhaps because the water seemed to be shimmering in a way I'd never seen before. I was not too drunk to realize I had a pretty fair chance of drowning if I actually dived in.

There was nothing else to do, so I just walked around. There were tons of good-looking young girls around the pool. About half of them were with guys who appeared to be about their age. Some were alone or with other girls, and the rest were all obviously younger than the men they were with. I hadn't noticed that when we'd arrived.

After a while—somewhere between ten minutes and an hour—I went back to the chairs and found Mr. Billionaire alone in his Speedo.

"Our wives came back and dragged Claire to get a manicure," he said. "I hope you don't mind, we invited her to join us tonight."

"I don't mind," I said. "What are we doing tonight?"

"Your speech," he said.

That's *right*—the accountants! I really needed to sober up. I thought maybe a nap would do the trick. I flopped down on the lounge chair and shut my eyes.

"I didn't know you were married before," I said.

"Oh, yes," he said. "For seventeen years."

"What happened?"

"People change," he said. "People move on."

"Yeah."

"Claire is a sweet kid, though," he said. "I never regret any of it because it's the reason I have her."

"It must be different doing it all over again," I said. "I mean, all these years later."

"You mean the kids?"

"Yeah."

"Well, Emmy really wanted them," he said, referring to his current wife. "I could have gone either way."

"I see."

"I'll tell you one thing, though," he said. "This time around, I haven't touched a diaper. I've been there, done that, if you know what I mean."

"I know what you mean."

It was right around then that I fell asleep.

Upon waking, I instantly realized that the last thing you want to do when you are drunk is fall asleep in the sun. My tongue felt like it was wrapped in cotton. My head was pounding. No one was around, which was something of a relief; I think if I'd seen Mr. Billionaire in his Speedo just then I'd have thrown up.

I made it to my room, where I filled a bucket with ice and shoved my head into it. That's where I am right now, chugging water and Gatorade. I think I'll be able to speak tonight, but my head still hurts and mostly that is making me cranky. And the more I think about the conversation we were having outside, the crankier it is making me.

I haven't touched a diaper. I've been there, done that.

Well, isn't that special?

Isn't that, in fact, the whole point? You *have* been there and done that. You are at the age where your daughter is *supposed* to be in law school, not nursery school. You are also at the age when it is common to be proud of your possessions, but children should not fall into that category.

Let me make my feelings perfectly clear: If you introduce me to your wife and your daughter, I shouldn't have to ask which is which.

If that isn't immediately evident, you are a lecherous jerk who should have bought a sports car instead of picking up your son's leftovers.

And, lest I forget, let's not let this trophy wife off the hook, either. She is a walking stereotype: a moneygrubbing blonde with a Gucci diaper bag who—in twenty years, when her husband is dead—will be complaining about men only being interested in women her daughter's age. That's life coming full circle, and it's as pathetic as it gets.

Then again, who am I to be judging anyone? Here I am, an hour away from two hundred accountants, and I've got my head buried in a bucket of ice because I got blind drunk at a swimming pool with a guy twenty years older than me whose nuts were hanging out. Obviously, I'm no angel. And I certainly have no right to tell people how to live their lives. But what frustrates me is the rationalization. I wish this guy would just admit what he is. Instead, he bullshits himself into believing he can be a good father again, and that his hottie *might* give him the time of day if he didn't drive a Porsche. He can't bullshit me, though, or the rest of the world, because we all see it for what it is.

Now, if you'll excuse me, I believe I have some throwing up to do.

The following day (still in Miami)

The speech went fine, all things considered. (By "all things," I mean that I threw up twice before the speech and then Mr. Billionaire walked into the room and I couldn't shake the image of his Speedo from my mind so I threw up two more times.)

By and large, though, the accountants seemed to like me and they laughed at all my jokes. Afterward the Billionaires joined us for a nice dinner, and following a good night's sleep I think I have recovered.

Then my wife and I went shopping, and I stepped right into a disaster that *could* have made the Billionaire's butt seem appealing by comparison. The fact that it did not end up that way—that I escaped fully unscathed—suggests I may really be learning. Or it could just be that I got very lucky. Either way, I can think of only one thing to say.

Phew, that was a close one.

It happened at Scoop, a very trendy clothing store in the Shore Club Hotel in South Beach. That it happened in Scoop is ironic, because that's the store I usually complain has the least comfortable seating.

I was shopping with my wife, as I always do because I enjoy buying clothes but I detest returning them; it helps cut out the middleman to find out that she hates the shirt before I've paid for it. The downside of shopping with my wife is that she *really* likes to shop. That is where we differ; I only like to buy. I walk into the store with a plan: try a few things on, make a decision, and get on with my life. I can usually make a pretty good haul in less than thirty minutes, including alterations.

My wife can't remove a hanger in thirty minutes. She takes her time when she shops, which is how I have come to judge stores based on the three S's.

1. Selection
2. Service
3. Seating

If you think I'm overstating the importance of the couches, you have definitely never been shopping with my wife. In her salad days, she could leave me seated for two hours. It is for that reason that I prefer department stores to boutiques. Neiman Marcus, for example, has a restaurant, multiple televisions, and endless reading material. The latest funky shop in SoHo, meanwhile, has a wooden bench and a two-year-old copy of *Vogue*, if you're lucky.

I guess I have come to judge stores based more on how pleasurable they are when you aren't shopping than when you are. I like the Prada store on Fifth Avenue, for example, because there is a glass elevator, unlimited refreshments, and excellent people watching. My all-time favorite is Mitchell's, in Connecticut, where they have self-service coffee and bagels, along with comfortable chairs and cable TV. I could kill an entire afternoon in that store. I know because I have, many times.

Scoop is not high on my list, but only for that reason; everything else about the experience is top-notch. I love the clothes and the service, but the moment my wife starts gabbing with the saleswoman about what Sarah Jessica Parker wore on *Sex and the City*, I'm doomed, because there is just nowhere good to sit.

When we entered this afternoon, I cursed myself for having forgotten to bring a book. An hour later, after I had picked out a pair of Joie's Bad Brain cords in brown, a James Perse washed cashmere sweater, and a John Varvatos suede belt, I was eyeing the hard-backed, wooden chairs and cursing even more loudly. Because my wife hadn't even started her engine. I knew that because she was still smiling. When she gets down to serious shopping, she always puts her game face on.

So I rifled through a small stack of magazines on the floor beneath the uncomfortable chairs. The best I could come up with was an old copy of *Glamour* that promised tips on how to have your greatest orgasm ever. In fact, I was so engrossed in that story that when the door to the dressing room opened I did not even look to see who was coming out. I kept on reading even as some woman began admiring herself in the mirror, which was situated directly beside my uncomfortable chair. Finally, something moved me to look up as this woman checked herself out in the mirror. And what I found was that this was no ordinary woman.

It was Elle Macpherson.

ELLE MACFUCKINGPHERSON!

She was so close, I thought she might ask me how she looked, which I'm glad she did not because I'm sure my response would have been unintelligible. I just sat there, mouth agape, and watched Elle Macpherson try on a pair of jeans. When she was finished, it was all I could do to keep from applauding. I just watched her walk back into the dressing room, which she did very slowly and God bless her for that. Then I looked around to see who else had noticed. This was a moment that had to be shared. Someone had to be around to have seen that.

And, of course, someone was.

"You can close your mouth anytime now."

I'll give you one guess who said that. I was sweating before she even asked the question.

"Do you really think she's that pretty?"

My mind went into overdrive. I could think of only two possible answers.

Honest: "OH MY GOD, YES! SHE'S OPERATING ON A WHOLE OTHER LEVEL! I'M NOT EVEN CONVINCED SHE'S A HUMAN BEING, I THINK SHE WAS SENT HERE FROM ANOTHER PLANET, WHERE THEY HAVE PERFECTED GENETIC ENGINEERING!"

Dishonest: "Not really."

I didn't see a winner either way, so I made a quick decision and split the difference.

"Yeah, she's very pretty," I said. "But not like she is in magazines. The way they airbrush those, they can make anyone look like a supermodel."

My wife just shrugged. "I think she's beautiful," she said, and left it at that.

Now, I know that isn't usually the end of it, so I remained on full alert for the entire drive home, ready for her to reinvent the topic in a subtle manner designed to catch me off guard.

It never happened.

In fact, it has now been almost ten hours and the issue has not been raised again. Maybe she's slipping. Or maybe I've learned something. Maybe the problem is that we husbands only talk ourselves into trouble when we're trying to talk ourselves out. Maybe the best answers to uncomfortable questions are always honest and subdued, like testimony on a witness stand: the truth, the whole truth, and nothing but the truth. No explanations, no rationalizations, no preemptive apologies. The more succinct you are, the less vulnerable you remain to cross-examination.

How about that? I think I'm getting somewhere. In fact, this has been quite a day. First, I score a pretty nice haul at Scoop. Then, I get to stare unabashedly at a supermodel at close range and suffer no consequences. And, finally, I learn fifteen ways to have the greatest orgasm ever. What more can you ask from a day than that?

•　　•　　•

For the first time in four years, my nephew Edgar spent the weekend with us. This time, with vastly different results. My lone recollection of his previous visit was of the stench. I am pleased to report that the boy no longer smells. Also, he has slowed considerably, to the point where my own children wore *him* out after a long Saturday afternoon. Sunday, Edgar spent with me. That was the whole point of the visit; today, I took the boy to his first football game.

His dad was supposed to do it but, last minute, he had to fly off to Hong Kong—or to Portland, I forget which—and he asked me to pinch-hit, which I was only too pleased to do. I enjoy spending time with Edgar now, mostly because, at the age of six, he already knows more about sports than I do.

The child is simply amazing; when it comes to sports he is a genuine prodigy. I doubt they test for that sort of thing, but if they did he'd obliterate the chess-playing kid from *Searching for Bobby Fischer*. I discovered this knowledge Friday night, which was also when I discovered that he can read. You see, I am wholly oblivious to the abilities of children older than mine. It had never occurred to me that a six-year-old was going to be able to read. Mostly, I was just relieved he could wipe his own behind. But there we were, in front of the television, watching *SportsCenter*, when he said to me, "Uncle Mike, LeBron James will make his NBA debut against the Sacramento Kings."

The picture on the television screen was of a baseball game, not basketball. They weren't talking about LeBron James at all. What could possibly have made Edgar say that?

Then I looked to the bottom of the screen and, sure enough, in the scrolling message they were promoting the much-anticipated debut of the young phenom.

"Did you read that off the television?" I asked Edgar.

"Yup."

"How long have you been able to read?"

"Long time."

"How long?"

"I think at least two weeks."

"I see," I said. "What does that say on there now?"

" 'Frank Thomas has exercised his option to return to the White Sox in 2004,' " he read.

"That's right," I said. This was fascinating. "What else can you read?"

"I don't know."

I grabbed a copy of *Newsweek* from off the kitchen counter. I pointed to the front-page headline. "What does that say?" I asked.

"I don't know."

"What do you mean?" I asked. It was in bold type, clear as a bell. DONALD TRUMP: TV'S GUILTY PLEASURE FOR A NERVOUS ECONOMY.

"I don't know," he said.

Then his mother came in and saw what was going on.

"He only reads sports," she said.

"What?"

"He only reads things that are about sports," she said. "Watch this."

She picked up a newspaper and turned to the front page, where there was a picture of Rush Limbaugh. "Edgar, what does this say?"

"I don't know, Mom."

Then she turned the paper around to the back page, with a picture of Derek Jeter. "What does this say?" she asked.

" 'Yankees Lose Series in Six,' " Edgar said. He took the newspaper from his mother and began reading aloud. " 'Josh Beckett tossed a complete-game, five-hit shutout, striking out nine, carrying the Marlins to a 2–0 blanking of the Yankees in Game Six of the World Series before a silenced crowd at Yankee Stadium. Beckett's masterpiece completed an improbable season for the Marlins, which culminated with the second World Series title in the franchise's eleven seasons.' "

I turned to the boy's mother. "Is there some medical diagnosis of this?"

"There is," she said. "It's called: He idolizes his Uncle Mike."

"That's very nice," I said. "But please tell me he can read other things, too."

"Of course he can," she said. "He just chooses not to."

Those were the last words she spoke to me before leaving the child in our care for the weekend, which passed happily and uneventfully until Sunday morning, when Edgar and I went off to the game.

In retrospect, perhaps the error was in the choice of game, though I do not fault the boy's father for that. Most people consider intracity rivalry games thrilling—they are consistently the toughest tickets to get. I understand he wanted his son's first game to be special, unforgettable. But what none of us—me included, and shame on me for it—had considered was the atmosphere in the stadium. This game was the New York Jets vs. the New York Giants, two teams that don't play each other often, so all the pent-up vitriol of their loyal fans—who often live in the same homes with one another—is spilled with great force on the rare occasions they meet. Such was the scene my six-year-old nephew and I innocently stumbled into this afternoon.

I gained my first sense of it in the parking lot. I am not accustomed to nearly so many cars bearing the colors of the opposing team; usually, there are hardly any. But today, it was split about fifty-fifty. Blue and Green. Giants and Jets. And the way it turned out, it might just as well have been Bloods and Crips.

I don't want to describe everything we saw and everything that happened, mostly because I just don't feel like reliving it, but suffice it to say my nephew had beer poured over his head before the opening kickoff. (My first thought was of how I would explain to his parents that I brought the boy home reeking of booze. Later, I realized that if I got the kid so drunk he forgot everything I might just be doing his family a favor.)

I gave up counting the number of times the word *fuck* was used within five feet of us by the middle of the first quarter. I gave up trying to cover his ears by halftime. And the third time a fight between drunken fans spilled into our row—my nephew's eyes widening in terror each time—we were on our way home. The fourth quarter hadn't begun, but we were finished. I didn't even know what the score was, and I didn't care. I just now heard on the radio that the Giants won in overtime.

C'est la vie.

As for Edgar, he was resilient, as I imagine most six-year-olds would be. He was visibly upset when we left, but the moment we got in the car all he talked about was what a great time it was. When we got home he told his mother it was the most fun he'd ever had.

I just left it at that.

There was no need for me to dispute his version of the afternoon, not for his sake or my own. But I did notice one interesting thing, when he sat down for a snack with my kids and picked up a box of crackers.

" 'Wheat Thins, ' " Edgar said, " 'for sensible snacking. A good source of calcium and fiber with no' . . . uh . . . Uncle Mike," he said, pointing to the box, "what is this word here?"

The word was "cholesterol." I tried to explain it to Edgar but that didn't go well, mostly because I have no idea how to explain what cholesterol is. But it also didn't go well because my mind wasn't really into the explanation. All I could think about was how well he had managed to read something other than sports once he had decided he wanted to.

Opening Monologue
The following day

I am nothing if not a man of the people. And by "the people," I'm talking about you. Because you're just like me. The only things separating us are a media credential and a parking pass.

I want to make life better for you, and my motivation is purely selfish; if life is better for you, and I am one of you, it stands to reason life is going to be better for me, too.

So today I want to talk about ways to make sports better for all of us. And let's not talk about any that are completely unrealistic. For example: ticket prices. They aren't coming down. I know you want them to and so do I, but it isn't going to happen, so let's move on.

Let's move to the subject of kidnapping. It's strange that kidnapping is a crime, but threatening to kidnap a sports franchise is not only legal, it has become standard operating procedure. You know what I'm talking about: The owner of a sporting franchise decides he wants a city or state to build him a new stadium so he threatens to move (kidnap) the team if he doesn't get his way. Come to think of it, that's not only kidnapping, it's extortion as well. But it happens all the time, and it works.

So my first proposal to make sports better is this: From this day forward, anyone wishing to purchase controlling interest in any sporting franchise must first sign an agreement stipulating that he will not relocate said franchise unless an independent arbitrator agrees there is no local buyer willing to offer fair market value.

(If that language sounded complicated, I'm thrilled. I wanted it to sound official, so I looked up a bunch of business terminology. In a nutshell, what it means is that no owner could move a team out of a city unless no one in that city wanted to buy it and keep it there.)

I don't think that is unrealistic, nor do I think it is unfair. In my opinion, owning a sports team is wholly different from owning any other kind of business. Civic pride and local identity are involved here, along with all those millions of dollars. I don't want to hear from any owner that he made an investment and thus can do whatever he wants—that's baloney. No one buys a team as an investment, mostly because it's a bad investment. There are an almost infinite number of better ways to invest that money. Billionaires buy ball clubs because it is exciting to be a part of sports. And that's fine, but with that prestige and visibility comes responsibility. That team matters to a whole lot of people, in a way no other business ever could. If I get my way, no owner will ever threaten to move a team again. And no kid will ever again wake up to find out his favorite team has fled.

That's a good start. I have a great many other ideas, which we'll get to over the course of time. There's no rush. This is a movement that is going to require a little patience.

It is also going to require some cooperation. As Jerry Maguire once said, I need you to help me help you. And there are two ways you can do that.

The first is to remember that as a sports fan you do not have to forfeit every shred of common sense you might apply to other areas of your life. You are a consumer, so how come you never behave like one? More often, you behave like a sheep. You follow blindly wherever your team leads you, no matter how preposterous the demands may be. You wouldn't spend seven dollars for twelve ounces of warm beer in a restaurant—why do you do it at a ball game? You wouldn't shop in a store where the staff treated you like a leper—why do you willingly accept rudeness and insults from ballplayers whose salaries you are paying? Do you see what I'm getting at here? The only way to restore sanity to sports is to demand that it be restored. If you don't do that then you cannot complain when they take advantage of you; it isn't a robbery when you willingly hand over your valuables to an unarmed man.

That's the first thing I need you to do. The second is just as easy. I need you to remember that it isn't about you.

No matter how much you love sports, and how far you inflate these games and players beyond any semblance of perspective, it isn't about you.

No matter how strongly you identify with your team or with the players, no matter how strongly your identity is based in your fandom, it isn't about you.

You are there to watch. You are not the show, no matter how badly you wish you could be.

If you remember that, it should help you to stop behaving as stupidly as you sometimes do. For goodness sakes, stop throwing beer on guys wearing the jerseys of the other team. Stop drinking so much before kickoff that your friends have to carry you to your seat. Stop screaming obscenities into the ears of little kids. For some, this is their first game. Stop ruining it.

Just remember that it isn't about you. If that makes you feel like a loser, take it up with a shrink or a clergyman or your wife; just quit punishing the rest of us because your life is empty.

If you'll do that for me, Lord knows what I may be able to do for you. Because at the end of the day, I am you. I'm a sports fan. I love my teams, I love my players, I love watching sports more than I love doing absolutely anything else. But it could be better. I'm going to try to make it better. For me and for you. Please, help me.

•   •   •

Today I almost got arrested for using the ladies' room. And the truth is, I would do it again. I used that ladies' room not just for me but for all men, all of us who've been treated as second-class citizens just because we are male. I used that ladies' room in order to shatter the glass ceiling that prevents us from becoming better fathers.

I did it for you, fellas.

Before I explain, I must first tell you about the time I went to see *Set It Off*, a pretty good movie with a predominantly black cast. I went with my friend Antoine, and while we were waiting for the lights to go out it struck me that I was the only white person in the theater. I mentioned this to Antoine in a whisper and he responded by laughing out loud.

"Now you know how *we* feel," he said.

I'll bet he doesn't even remember saying that, but ever since then I have been acutely aware of just how often there is only one black person someplace. When you are white and male, you spend just about your whole life in the majority. That movie theater was one exception. My life as a dad has been another.

You see, the greatest benefit of hosting morning-drive radio is that I am home so early. I think I spend more time with my kids than any dad I know, which is terrific. Consequently, I am also the only man almost every place I go, and frankly that can suck.

When I take my kids to playgroups, it is always three moms and me; at the park, twenty moms and me; shopping, two hundred moms and me. And all the moms look at me funny. (You see, not one of these women knows who I am. The demographics of sports radio do not include many full-time moms. I am sure there are stations that air only static with more female listeners than I have; I'll never forget one woman who asked for my autograph and then said, "I just know my husband and sons are going to be excited. Now, tell me who you are again.") The women in town see me pushing a stroller in the middle of the afternoon and I can see in their faces that they have me pegged.

A stay-at-home dad? I would sooner sleep with the lone male member of my book club!

You can't miss it, and no matter how good you feel about yourself you cannot pretend it doesn't exist. No matter how cute my kids are, or how satisfied I feel at the end of a day with them, there is still a place inside where I cry out every time a woman looks at me like I'm a male cheerleader.

You don't understand! I'm just done for the day! I have a job! I'm the reason you roll your eyes in the car every morning because your husband forces you to listen to me instead of your Gwen Stefani CD!

Today was one of those days.

It was a crisp, sunny afternoon, cold but not enough that I couldn't take my son out for a walk. We went to Main Street, where I paraded him up and down in a stroller. I kept feeling his cheeks to see if he was too cold and he never seemed to be, but after twenty minutes I saw that his fingers had turned red; I had forgotten his mittens. No problem. There is a Gymboree at the end of the street. I would have him nice and toasty in two minutes.

On the way, I passed two great-looking moms drinking gourmet coffee. They paused as I passed and gave me that little nod I have become used to.

Nice looking kid, Nancy-boy.

I didn't have time to worry about it, though. I had an infant with frosty fingers. Into Gymboree I went, a store I have been in a hundred times before. (My daughter and I took these same walks when she was a baby; I know every crack in the sidewalk.) I even remembered where they kept the mittens and I looked there; then I thought of a few places they might have moved them to and I looked there, but I couldn't find any. So I went to the saleswoman, who was chatting with two moms by the overalls. I could see them size me up as I pushed my stroller toward them.

We would sooner have sex with Barney the Purple Dinosaur.

"Excuse me," I said, "I'm trying to find some mittens."

The saleswoman looked over to the two women as though she was waiting for them to help me. "Are they for you or the baby?" she finally asked, and the three of them cackled.

"They're for him," I said, and spun the carriage around so they could see my son, who had just fallen asleep.

"He's cute," said one of the mothers.

"You really should cover up his hands," said the other. "They're freezing."

"That's why I'm here," I said. "I'm trying to get him some mittens."

"We don't have mittens," the saleswoman said.

"You're out of them?"

"No, we don't carry mittens," she said. "Only gloves."

Now, I know I bought my daughter a pair of mittens in that store. I vividly remember them: pink with little pom-poms. They got lost on a trip to Aspen.

"Maybe I'll just look around a little," I said.

Then I tried to push the stroller away, but I got stuck. I had managed to wedge myself into a tight lane and I tried to make a three-point turn, but it just wasn't happening. The women were standing there, staring, and the pressure began to mount, like when you try to park on a busy street and everyone is honking. I could feel them staring until sweat broke out under my woolen cap. Finally, the carriage was out of the aisle and I made my escape, looking just to get as far away as I could.

"Thank you," I shouted, halfheartedly.

"Don't forget to ask your wife if he can wear gloves instead of mittens!"

I stopped dead when the saleswoman said that.

As I look back now, reading the words over, they appear harmless. But in the moment, they did not. They said I was incapable of making that decision. They said only a woman could know if gloves would suffice. They said I wasn't able to take care of my kid solely because I am a man. As I look back, maybe they didn't really mean any of that. But at the moment, they pissed me off.

I was in a full sweat when I exited, angry. My son was snoozing, blissfully oblivious, so I just walked up Main Street, muttering to myself.

Yes, you DID sell mittens! I bought a pair! I KNOW you sell mittens!

Pretty soon the little guy's fingers were turning red again and I wanted to get him indoors so I headed to the library, which I adore. My daughter actually took her first steps in the library, pulling herself to her feet on the bottom shelf of a bookcase. And she spoke her first words there, too ("Sam, I am"). She used to sit on my lap and read

Green Eggs and Ham while we watched the ducks swim past outside the window. If any destination might calm my nerves *and* warm my son's fingers, the library was it.

The little guy woke up as soon as we got inside, which was great, then immediately did something in his diaper, which was not as great. The odor overwhelmed the espresso bar. There was no way any patron of the library was going to enjoy the afternoon if someone didn't do something.

I was prepared, as always, with all the necessities neatly stored in my Prada backpack: diapers, wipes, Balmex, waterless soap, change of clothes, plastic garbage bag. All I needed was a changing table.

That's where the trouble began.

I have been in that men's room a hundred times and never noticed that there is no changing table in there. I suppose it is like a refrigerator humming—you never notice until it isn't there. Today I noticed.

So that's the scenario: I'm carrying my son as lovingly as one can carry an infant at full arm's length—already in a bad mood because of the emasculating mothers and patronizing saleswoman—and now there is a hideous odor emanating from the seat of his pants and I have nowhere to change him.

I went to the desk and expressed my concern.

"Oh, dear," said the librarian, "we've never had a changing table in there."

"Why not?"

"We just never saw the need for one."

"Then where can I change him?"

"Well," she said, "the only changing table is in the ladies'."

"There is no gender-neutral site where I can change this child?"

"I'm sorry."

"Then I'm just going to have to use the ladies' room," I said. "Please go in there and tell everyone I'll be as quick as I can."

"I'm sorry," she said, "I can't authorize that. Only the library manager can authorize that. You'll have to speak with her."

"I'd like to."

"I'm afraid she isn't here," she said. "She'll be in first thing in the morning. Would you like me to make an appointment for you?"

"No, I do not want to speak to the manager tomorrow about my son's diaper. I am going into the ladies' room and that's all there is to it."

Off I went, feeling a lot like Norma Rae. I gave the door three loud kicks and then barged in, despite the protestation of the librarian, whose bouffant hairdo I was on the verge of mocking.

I'll say this: The ladies' room is the most obdurately foreign place I have ever been. It felt different being in there. It felt wrong, like when I was a teenager and used to sneak into the lingerie section at Bloomingdale's to ogle the bras. But then my son was kicking me in the ribs and I realized I'd better get down to business. I changed the child as quickly as I could, and as I pulled his pants back on, I was sure I had pulled off a coup.

Then I saw the cop waiting for me outside.

I don't mean outside the library, I mean outside the door of the ladies' room—a smile on his mustachioed lips, a gun in his holster.

"What exactly do you think you were doing in there, sir?"

I would love to tell you I stood tough, refused to answer questions, and swore to the cop he'd never take me alive. But I did not. Instead I launched into an incoherent monologue about how unfair it was that there was nowhere for a man to change a baby, and that I'd contributed thousands of dollars to the library, and that the women on Main Street were mean. Then, just as I was on the verge of demanding my Miranda rights, the officer cut me off.

"Aren't you the guy from the radio?"

Yes! I am the guy from the radio! Please tell me that means I can use the ladies' room if I want to!

"I listen to your show every morning," the cop said. "I'm also a big Jets fan."

"I'm so glad to meet you," I said, turning the stroller so he could see the Jets hat on my infant's head. "I'm sorry if I've created a stir around here."

"Well, I understand your frustration," he said, "but that doesn't mean you can just barge into the ladies' room. What if there would have been women in there? We could have really had some trouble here."

"I fully understand that. I can't tell you how embarrassed I am."

"I'm going to let you go, but I don't think you should come back in here for a while," he said. "An apology to the librarian might not hurt either."

"Absolutely," I said, nodding. "You bet I will."

"All right, Mr. Greenberg, you take care of that little guy. Make sure *he* knows which bathroom to use."

I shook his hand as firmly as I could and then he was gone. I looked over at the librarian and saw that her bouffant was a tad askew. I suppose a man barging into the ladies' room qualifies as quite a commotion in the library. I didn't apologize to her, though.

With my head held high I pushed my little boy to the door and back outside, where the sun was setting and the air felt ten degrees colder. It was quite chilly now and I still didn't have any mittens, so I really needed to get home. I walked quickly to the car, defiantly meeting the eye of every woman who passed, and as I strapped the little guy into his car seat, I felt proud of what I had done. I had actually taken a stand, or as close to a stand as I have ever taken. And I wasn't sorry at all. My only regret is that my son and I won't be hanging out together in the library like my daughter and I did. That is a shame. I guess he'll have to say his first words someplace else.

*   *   *   *

Well, he said them in Colorado.

The good news is we know what his first words are now. The bad news is we're surely not going to record them, or even write them down. Nor are we excitedly calling the grandparents, or even encouraging the child to talk more. Mostly, we are just horrified.

My son's first words are: "Oh shit."

This is a tragedy. Not only because they are the only words he has ever spoken, but because now he runs around saying them all the time. The only thing that could make this worse is if it was my fault, and of course it was. So I am really down.

It happened in Aspen, of all places, where we were skiing over the weekend with friends. We go every year. There used to be six of us; now there are sixteen of us. (Three couples, three nannies, seven kids.) We rent one big house with cathedral ceilings three stories high. I can't imagine how they change the lightbulbs.

Bad place to play with helium balloons, but we did anyway. We brought them home for the kids, and I was holding my son's green one by the string when it accidentally slipped through my fingers. I jumped to catch it but couldn't, and as I watched it drift toward the ceiling I spoke the only words that came to mind.

"Oh shit!"

Then I looked down at the boy, ashamed I'd sworn in front of him. And he smiled angelically and spoke his first words.

"Oh shit."

They came out oddly, in one continuous syllable, but clear as can be.

Of course, all the adults cracked up simultaneously, and before we could stop ourselves we had convinced the boy that this was the greatest achievement of his life. Now he is hooked; no matter how I try to convince him otherwise, he believes "oh shit" is the coolest thing in the world.

So those will always be his first words. Not "Mama" or "Dada" or "milk" or "juice" or even my daughter's first words, "Sam, I am." He has begun his vocabulary with an expletive, and it is mostly my fault. Consequently, I was feeling pretty lousy on the flight home, even before he showed off his new skill for everyone on the plane. (That was the most stunned I have ever seen a flight attendant look.)

And, as only she can, my wife made me feel infinitely worse. "Look at the bright side," she said. "Conversationally speaking, he has no-where to go from here but up."

So, that was my weekend. Perhaps it was still cluttering my mind at the meeting today. I'm not sure what other excuse I can give, aside from my son's potty mouth, for how woefully wrong this thing went. And it wound up costing me fifty grand.

Here's what happened: My agent set up a meeting with an auto company that I will not name in case they read this. They wanted to do a campaign for their car: "Rugged enough for a jock, but stylish enough for his wife to drive." A terrific idea; I was perfect for it.

The meeting started great. My agent led me into a conference room, where we found two guys from the auto company, plus a man and woman from the ad agency and another woman from the media-buying firm. I gave them all an up-and-down. Among the men, one was wearing an Italian suit and Gucci shoes, the second an inexpensive suit with a mismatched tie, and the third a rumpled sports jacket with a mustard stain on the lapel. Both women were tastefully dressed.

Now that I had the lay of the land, it was time to begin.

I opened with self-deprecating humor: "I was so unpopular growing up, my only friends were imaginary!"

Then I segued into a few jokes about my rotund partner: "He's so fat and I'm so thin, standing next to each other we look like the number ten!"

And I finished with a thoughtful remark: "My philosophy is, 'Take your job seriously, not yourself!' "

It was perfect. The ice was successfully broken, the deli tray was wheeled in, and the guy with the mustard stain was slurping coffee so loudly he drowned out the street noise. Then I heard somebody ask if beer was available, and my agent started throwing down corned beef like he hadn't eaten in a month. Meanwhile, I had my arm casually around one of the guys as he shared the story of his first visit to Yankee Stadium. (Sports fans live to tell me about their first trips to Yankee Stadium. Usually I can do without it, but if this guy was paying me fifty grand I was willing to order transcripts.)

I was so relaxed I ventured toward the deli tray. Normally I don't eat at these things, because it is my job to be talking and someone always manages to ask an important question just as I am shoveling in cole slaw. But this deal was done.

I helped myself to turkey and cheese, and then, with the mustard-stained guy beside me, I took the spoon out of the tuna salad and offered it to him. But the spoon slipped through his fingers and clanged to the ground, loudly enough to stop the whole room, despite the carpet.

"Oh shit."

That was me. I knew immediately I shouldn't have said it; nothing could be less appropriate in this setting. It's just that my son has been saying it seven thousand times a day, so it must be stuck in my brain. I needed to say something else, if only to put different words into the air.

"I mean, oopsy daisy."

Worse. That's another phrase I use with my kids, but as I looked about the room I realized it was an unusual thing for a grown man—especially a sportscaster—to say. I glanced at my agent, who had frozen mid-bite on a triple-decker sandwich; I was destroying the vibe. There was an awkward silence in the room. I really needed to say something else.

"Boy, that must have made me sound like a pussy!"

Are you kidding? A guy who makes his living thinking on his feet comes up with that?

"I'm sorry, everybody, it's been a long week," I said, sheepishly. "Enjoy your lunch."

The room was so quiet I think I heard my agent gulp. Everyone ate in silence for just a few more minutes, and then one by one they got out of Dodge. The first to go was the classier-looking of the two women. "It has certainly been a pleasure meeting you," she said.

"We'll be in touch soon with a decision." (Translation: *Tell your agent to eat up because the corned beef is all you're getting out of this.*)

Next was the well-dressed fellow, who extended his hand. "Pleasure," he said, without smiling. "We'll be in touch."

Last up was mustard boy. "Take care," he said, extending a greasy palm. "And a little advice: Clean it up around the ladies."

It was a bloodletting.

Ten minutes after "oh shit" and "oopsy daisy," my agent and I were alone in the room. With nothing else to do, I piled a plate high with cold cuts and sat beside him.

"That was well played," he said. "Next time you might want to save 'pussy' for after the papers have been signed."

"I couldn't live with 'oopsy daisy,' " I said. "I couldn't just leave it out there."

"Where the hell did you get 'oopsy daisy,' anyway?" he asked. "I've never heard you say 'oopsy daisy.' "

"That's because you've never been at the house when the kids are building with blocks."

We ate in silence a few minutes.

"Let me ask you a question," I finally said. "Do we have any conceivable chance of getting this deal?"

"You have a better chance of collecting fifty thousand dollars' worth of aluminum cans and turning them in for the deposit."

"Because I said 'pussy'?"

"That is correct," he said.

"Let me ask you this," I said. "If I had left 'oh shit' and 'oopsy daisy' out there, what would have happened?"

He just shook his head.

"You know, my son's first words were 'Oh shit,' " I said.

"I'm not surprised to hear that."

"How old are *your* kids again?" I asked him.

"Nineteen and sixteen."

"Do you ever find yourself using their lingo in an inappropriate setting?"

"I haven't understood a fucking word either of them has said in five years."

We ate in silence awhile longer. I was in no hurry to get home. I need to spend more time around adults, anyway. I really do.

· · ·

Or maybe I don't.

Maybe once again I have things perfectly backward. Maybe it is not *less* time I need to spend with my children, it is *more*. I was reminded of that again today, appropriately so after my idiocy yesterday. (I don't mean what I said at the meeting. I mean what I wrote afterward. Imagine the nerve of me, to think I could ever learn as much from a car salesman as I can from my kids.) Thankfully, just when such nonsense crosses my mind, my kids always have a way of teaching me lessons worth much more than fifty thousand dollars.

Like this afternoon, when I picked up my daughter from nursery school. That is the moment in my day I most look forward to. I always arrive early so I can watch through the door; I love the way they play. I love the way the girls' dresses twirl, I love the way the boys wrestle, I love the way they all tell secrets even though they don't know what secrets are. (All they know is they are told urgently in a hushed voice with a hand cupped over the mouth; this leads to such secrets as "Taylor likes potato chips.")

Once the other parents begin to arrive, I make myself visible in the doorway and wait until she sees me. That's the best part. Every day it is as though my presence is the greatest surprise she's ever had. That is a lesson I could take from her. Imagine how much happier I would be if the moments I have come to count on never lost their magic.

Today, she was skipping out the door with Renee and Jessica when one of the girls slipped and scraped her knee. (I think it was Jessica. I'm still working on telling them apart.)

"Just like at recess," my daughter said.

"What did you do at recess?" I asked.

"Me and Renee and Taylor ran and the boys chased us," she said.

"We don't like boys," said the other little girl.

I turned to see if her mother was stunned, but she didn't bat an eye. I was a bit taken aback; I didn't realize they even knew the difference between girls and boys. Must be the separate bathrooms.

In the car, I asked my daughter more about recess.

"Honey, do you play nicely with the boys?"

"Sometimes," she said, fiddling with her seat belt, "but not too much."

That's the same answer she gives when I ask if she loves her little brother. Just now, all she wanted was the ice cream I'd promised her last night.

"I'll have vanilla," she told the lady at Baskin-Robbins, "with rainbow sprinkles on top and a cone on the bottom."

I love how my daughter orders ice cream.

Then we were back in the car and I was trying to keep the sprinkles from spilling on her dress. "Honey, did anything exciting happen today at school?"

"Not too much," she said. "I'm marrying Casten."

Please let that be a girl.

"Who is Casten?" I asked, trying my best to maintain a normal tone.

"He's in my class."

I know my wife would say it was cute to hear little girls talk that way, but just then my instinct was to drive into the path of an oncoming truck.

"What do you mean you are marrying him?" I asked.

"I don't know."

"*When* are you marrying him?"

"I don't know."

"*Why* are you marrying him?"

She just looked at me. It was a look I recognized—her mother uses it all the time. It told me to shut up because she was trying to eat her ice cream and this was a harmless game four-year-olds play, and for me to make a fuss only proved they were more mature than I am. She reminds me more of her mother every day. Except for the sprinkles; my wife prefers chocolate.

After the ice cream we went to the flower shop, which is my daughter's favorite place. There is a little cat named Thomas that she calls Tommy because it is so small, and once there was a litter of kittens and they let my daughter hold one and I've never seen her so happy. But the cats aren't the reason we go.

She loves the flowers. They are her passion; they are to her what shoes are to her mother. And you have not lived until you have sniffed flowers with a four-year-old girl. It is a transcendent experience.

"The roses smell like cherry, Daddy, because they are red, but the violets smell better because purple is my favorite color."

You should know that the yellow ones smell different from the orange ones, too. Most days the aroma of the flowers can take the edge off anything. But today I was still a little uptight when it was time to go. I guess I've been a little uptight a lot lately. So I took her by the hand and we waved to Tommy the cat and we were going to the car when my daughter just stopped.

"Daddy," she said, pulling her hand away, "you're walking too fast."

She was right, of course. She always is. I *am* walking too fast.

"I'm sorry, honey," I said, and picked her up. "I'll slow down."

It isn't a good idea to be in a hurry all the time. It makes the weeks go by too fast. It makes Friday feel like the day after Monday, and then months and years and life is racing away. Maybe it doesn't matter so much when meetings end badly, even if they end with a foot in my mouth and my agent choking on corned beef. Maybe what I really need to do is pay more attention to how different the purple flowers smell from the yellow ones. Maybe what children do is slow down time. There is so much I can learn from my little girl. I hope to be just like her someday.

Redemption

Opening Monologue
Monday, December 8

I saw something that made me really sad yesterday.

It was one of those things you hear about all the time but never think could actually happen where you live, among people you know. It was the sort of thing that always happens somewhere else, far away, someplace you are ready to dismiss as being unenlightened, the sort of place where they have Elvis sightings and UFO landings. But this wasn't there, this was here. Right where I live. Among people I know. And it was difficult to watch.

It was at a ball game. I've been to thousands of ball games in my life and one of the things you become accustomed to is belligerent fans. We've all dealt with them, whether they are sitting nearby, shouting obscenities into your ears, or across the way, starting fights that cause entire sections to deflect their attention from the game.

Well, there was one of those fans at this ball game, but he wasn't drunk. He didn't have his face painted or his shirt off. In fact, he was nicely dressed, in a sports jacket and slacks and a tie that I'm pretty sure was Hermès. And he wasn't vulgar. He didn't use any language that was unsuitable for young ears, which was a good thing because there were a lot of young ears around.

I know the guy, actually; he's a successful lawyer. He lives just a few houses away from me. I once helped him get a pair of tickets to a basketball game and he sent me a case of Hangar One vodka—my favorite—in appreciation. So he has manners, and he has money, but he doesn't have class. I found that out yesterday.

We were at this game, and he was riding the umpire, mercilessly. I don't know that five minutes ever went by that he didn't strenuously object to something the umpire had done. And there weren't many spectators at this game, so everyone could hear every word.

Then the guy turned his attention to one of the players, and he was even less delicate than he had been with the umpire. Apparently, this one player was out of position on every play. And he didn't hustle. And then once he stopped to wave to his mother, and the guy in the stands told him he would not be allowed to play anymore if he didn't keep his head in the game.

All of this might be considered no big deal at most baseball games, but in this case the game was T-ball, and the players were four years old, and the one kid this guy was riding was his own son.

You hear about this sometimes, about the fathers at their kids' hockey games that come to blows, or the mothers who pull their kids off the tennis court because of an unfavorable call from a line judge, but you don't ever expect to see it. Not in your own neighborhood. Not from a lawyer in a hundred-dollar tie.

If this story sickens you a little, I've done my job. Hell, I'm a little queasy just telling it. It was like the scene in *Bad News Bears* where the opposing manager smacks his own son on the field. Only it wasn't as dramatic without the music from *Carmen*, or as funny without Walter Matthau.

Anyway, it made me think about what we can do, all of us together, to keep this sort of thing from happening anymore. And I think I've come up with something.

Here goes:

If you are a parent and your children are playing sports, when they come home from their next game don't ask them if they won. Instead, try a different question.

"Did you have fun?"

Let them decide when to tell you if they won or lost. Maybe it will take longer than you expect. Maybe it won't be among the first things they mention. Maybe your son will tell you how good the popcorn smelled. Maybe your daughter will tell you about the way her heart was beating when she took a lead off first base and saw the manager give the steal sign. Maybe your son will be upset with himself because he lost a pop fly in the sun, or maybe he'll be excited because that really pretty Michelle Nussbaum was watching and she waved at him when the game ended.

Maybe your kids will really surprise you and go upstairs to wash up without ever telling you who won. Maybe it isn't as important to them as it is to you.

Of course, it's possible that none of those things will happen. Maybe the first words out of his mouth will be: "We stomped them into submission! We put our feet on their throats and never let them breathe!" Or maybe she'll come home and say: "We lost and as a result my life lacks all meaning."

Those are probably just as likely as anything I suggested. I guess it's up to you. But here's what I'm going to do: When my daughter and I play Old Maid this afternoon, I'm not going to let her win. I just hope she beats me anyway. And, more than that, I hope that whichever way it goes she wants to play again tomorrow.

· · ·

Went to see Dr. Gray today, told her about what happened when I was trying to leave the house. It was last week, when I had to go on the road. I was going for five days, the longest I've been away in a while, and feeling blue about it. Maybe that rubbed off on the kids; I think they pick up on things like that, like dogs do. Either way, I explained to them that Daddy had to take a little trip and that he'd be back soon. I told them I'd call every day while I was gone.

Immediately, my daughter started crying.

"Daddy," she said, "I don't want you to go."

Then my son started to cry, not because he had any idea I was leaving but because he does everything his big sister does.

"I don't want to go either," I said, squeezing them both, "but the good news is, I'll be home really soon."

"I'm going to miss you," my daughter said, between sobs.

She barely got the words out through her tears. She can be a bit dramatic, probably because she knows it works.

"I'm going to miss you too," I said, "but it's okay to miss each other."

"Oh, Daddy," my daughter said, collapsing in a heap on the couch.

So my son collapsed too, in the exact same position. Then the car was waiting to take me to the airport. I kissed my wife on the lips.

"I'll miss you, too," she said.

She looked like she meant it. Then my daughter was racing toward me from the couch.

"Daddy!" she yelled.

And, of course, her brother was right behind her.

"Da-da!"

So I was on my knees, squeezing them both, and I turned and kissed the little girl on her cheek.

"Daddy," she said, "I'm really going to miss you."

I gave the little boy a kiss, too.

"Da-da," he said, "petzools, cup."

He was telling me he wanted pretzels, in a cup. His talking is really coming along.

"Mommy will get you some," I said, and gave them both another squeeze.

When I recounted the story for Dr. Gray this morning, I couldn't stop shaking my head. "My kids are really something," I said. "*She* is going to miss me, *he* wants pretzels in a cup."

"Isn't that wonderful?" she asked.

"I don't know how wonderful it is," I said, "to walk out the door when the kids are both crying."

"It may be tough but it should also be wonderful," she said.

"I don't find it especially wonderful."

"Michael," she said, "those kids are going to be grown up and you won't believe how much you'll miss them crying when you walk out the door."

"I guess so."

"Let me tell you something," she said. "The greatest frustration of getting older is when you begin to miss things that you didn't enjoy when they were happening. If you look up the word *regret* in the dictionary, that's what it should say."

I nodded. Actually, I nodded for a long time. And as soon as we were done with the session I jotted the words down. They seem worth remembering. In all the years I've been going to see Dr. Gray that was the first thing she ever told me that I didn't already know.

●　●　●

Today I cried in front of two men I do not know.

I'll be curious to see if Dr. Gray thinks *that* should have been wonderful, too. I certainly didn't think so. It isn't something I'd ever thought I'd do. And it was an accident, in the way that all things are accidents when you are a little famous. It was an accident that began three and a half years ago, when I took my daughter to her first swimming lesson.

I'll never forget trying to put her bathing suit on that first time. I'll also never forget when I discovered the urine. She was six months old and we were waiting to get into the pool, watching the class before ours finish up, when one child caught my eye, an oversized blond boy who had been crying throughout the class and now his mother was dragging him out of the pool and there was no mistaking the fact that the kid was peeing as he went. Flat-out peeing. No effort was made to hide it or stop it, just walking and crying and peeing at the same time.

Had I the authority, I would have banished the family from our town.

I picked my daughter up and went to the lifeguard to voice my disgust.

"Excuse me," I said. "I don't mean to be indelicate, but that little boy was clearly peeing in the pool."

"I'm sorry, what?" she asked.

"I know it's disgusting, but that kid was peeing right in the pool. I don't know if there is something you need to do."

She did something, all right. She burst out laughing.

"I don't understand what you find so funny," I said.

"Sir," she said, "this water is a hundred degrees and these are babies. What do *you* think is going on in there?"

"You aren't trying to tell me that all these kids are peeing in this pool," I said.

"That's *exactly* what I'm telling you," she said. "Every kid, including yours."

I became indignant. "Now you listen, my little girl is not peeing in this pool."

"If she's not," the lifeguard said, lifting the whistle to her mouth, "she's the only one who isn't." She blew a shrill blast to begin our first class. "We're starting, sir. Time to get in."

By the end of that lesson, I was ready to cry. Every time a kid splashed near me I was apoplectic. I waded over to the lifeguard and begged for help.

"How do you handle this?" I asked.

"I've been doing it for five years."

"That isn't an answer," I said. "How can you swim in here knowing all the kids are peeing?"

"Mister," she said, "I guarantee you someone has peed in every pool you've ever swum in. That's why there are chemicals in the water. There is so much chlorine in this pool right now that if you went under and opened your eyes they would be red for a week."

Just then there was less chance of me putting my head under the water than there was of my daughter doing the butterfly all the way to the deep end.

"What's your name, mister?" the lifeguard asked.

"Michael."

"Listen, Michael," she said. "Nothing bad is going to happen to her in this water."

As it turned out, I grew accustomed to the pool over time and even made peace with the urine. Weeks went by, then months, and then years, and for all the things that changed in our lives, I always had Sunday mornings in that pool with my little girl.

Until today.

We arrived fifteen minutes before the start of class. She put on her bathing suit—she does that herself these days—and I put on mine. Then I took her by the hand and we made our way down the chilly tiled hall. We pushed open the door and there was the same lifeguard who has been with us every Sunday for all these years.

"Hey, Michael," she yelled to me, "why are you in your bathing suit?" Then she came over and took my daughter's hand. "Your silly daddy," she said. "Doesn't he know that now that you are four, this is a drop-off class?"

I didn't.

"That's right, Michael," the lifeguard said. "See you in a half hour."

"I can't even watch?"

"I need you to go," she said. "We find it much harder if moms and dads are here."

She started leading my daughter away.

"But . . . wait."

Then my baby was at the edge of the pool with two of her friends. One of them made her laugh and she looked up and saw me and waved. "Bye, Daddy!"

"See that?" the lifeguard said. "She doesn't need you anymore."

I went back to the locker room and got dressed very slowly. Then I sat down on the floor. There just wasn't anywhere for me to go. I don't know what the rest of the world does on Sunday mornings, but I take my daughter swimming.

There were a few high school kids hanging around; I was used to seeing them. They play basketball on Sunday mornings and they all listen to my radio show, so they usually chat me up and they're always cute with my little girl. With nothing better to do, I figured I would go watch them play.

I did manage to get lost in their game. The kids were high-fiving after every basket and shouting at me to talk about them on the radio. That was fun. Then they took a water break, and one of them stopped to talk to me.

"Hey, where's your little girl?" he asked.

"She's at her swimming lesson."

"Don't I always see you swimming with her?"

"Yeah," I said. "But she doesn't need me anymore."

Because there is mercy in the universe, the kid decided he was too thirsty to continue talking. His drink of water is the only reason he didn't see me burst into tears.

All I could think to do was get the hell out of that gym.

Thankfully I made it, and then I was outside on a bright, sunny morning, and I wished for my sunglasses. With nowhere to go I sat on the steps of the YMCA and tried to regain my composure. It was an awkward cry, as most of mine are. Men do not cry as well as women, perhaps because we so seldom do it. Our trouble is that we fight it. I think if we would just let it come it would be over more quickly.

Then an unfamiliar voice asked a very familiar question.

"Hey, aren't you the sports guy?"

I looked up to find two guys right in my face.

Of course I am. Who else would be sitting here crying in front of the YMCA?

"Hey, Greeny," one of them said, "are you all right?"

"I'm fine."

"Do you need anything?" the other asked.

"I'm just having a tough day."

They didn't leave.

"Hey, would you mind signing my ball?"

It was the second guy who asked, the one who'd wanted to know if I needed anything. I hadn't noticed that he was holding a football.

"Sure," I said.

They looked at each other awkwardly, then back at me. I knew it before they said it. They didn't have a pen.

"I'm sure someone has a pen inside," the first one said.

"That's fine," I said.

The second fellow was standing at the door. "Would you mind coming in?"

In the next five minutes, I signed the football and both of their T-shirts and left a message on the answering machine of one guy's boss. Then they were off, into the gym, carrying the football I had signed. It was the first time in my life that being a little famous had been an intrusion. But I'm glad I was nice to them anyway. They would have told everyone I was a jerk if I hadn't been. And you can't blame them, really; they had no way of knowing this was the most wistful morning of my life.

Soon it was time to pick up my daughter.

She took her own hot shower and washed her hair and dressed herself and cheerfully told me she was hungry, so I took her by the hand and we went for lunch. While she ate she told me a funny story about something she saw on television, something about a frog kissing an apple and turning into a princess. I think she got it a little mixed up. But it was funnier the way she told it anyway, and she got peanut butter all over her face and some in her hair when she was laughing. And I laughed too. And Dr. Gray was right. There *was* something wonderful about it. Then my daughter told me, excitedly, that she had jumped into the pool without anyone to catch her. And I told her I was proud of her. But what I didn't tell her was that, in a way, I already knew she had.

* * * *

Well, this was officially the strangest day of my life. (And that includes the summer I spent traveling with the Ramones.)

I had just finished the radio show and I had a lot of messages waiting when I turned on my cell phone. One of them was from my aunt.

"Michael, I need to talk to you. Call me as soon as you can."

Something in her tone told me she meant it this time.

"Darling, great to hear from you," she said when I called. "I need injury reports desperately."

"Ada, I'll do them on the show Friday, like I always do."

"That's no good," she said. "I'll be in Puerto Rico on my honeymoon Friday. I need to give Fern Cohen my picks today."

"I'm sorry, Ada. What did you just say?"

"Fern says I can call in my picks from Puerto Rico, but do you have any idea what that would cost me?"

"Aunt Ada, let's start this all over again. Where are you going to be on Friday?"

"Weren't you listening? I'm going to be in Puerto Rico."

"Why are you going to Puerto Rico?"

"Because I was just in Vegas and the Virgin Islands are a little pricey."

"Aunt Ada, did you just say you were going on a honeymoon?"

"Yes, darling, I'm leaving Thursday morning."

"When are you getting married?"

"What time is it now?"

She managed to answer even that with a question.

"You're getting married today?"

"Yes, darling, in about a half hour."

"Where?"

"Here, at the house."

"You're getting married in a half hour in your apartment in Flushing?"

"That's right," she said. "Now, what are you hearing about Tom Brady's wrist?"

"He's going to play," I said. "Who are you marrying?"

"Alan Glickstein," she said. "How about LaDainian Tomlinson's ankle?"

"I wouldn't count on him. Who the hell is Alan Glickstein?"

"He's the man I've been dating for three years. Is Randy Moss going to play?"

"No, lay off the Vikings," I said. "Why didn't I know you were dating someone for three years?"

"What do you think, you know *everything*?"

"Ada, hold on. I'm on my way over."

It was a disappointment that I had to go alone, but my wife had a meeting and my daughter was on a field trip and my son had just gone down for a nap, and I didn't want to disrupt everyone's day for a wedding to which we hadn't been invited in the first place.

But I was going.

When I walked into the apartment, I was stunned. First, with the size of the crowd; there must have been two dozen people in the one-bedroom flat. Next, I was stunned by the age of the crowd. I think I was the only one who wasn't eighty.

"Aunt Ada," I shouted from the doorway, struggling to maneuver through the packed house. "I'm here."

I saw her wave to part the crowd. "My nephew is here," she said, shooing away people I had never seen before. "Come in, Michael."

She led me through the octogenarian sea until we made it to the bedroom, where we found a distinguished-looking gentleman wearing a navy sports jacket and tan slacks. His appearance was disarming in that he looked so normal; his normalcy seemed completely out of place.

"Michael," he said, extending a warm handshake, "I've heard so much about you. Your aunt is very special to me. I'm a lucky man."

"I'm going to get some of the girls in here to say hello," Ada said. "Then we'll get started. I have a brisket in the oven, so I need everyone out by five."

"It is such a pleasure to meet you," Alan said, when we were alone. "Your aunt is very proud of what a big star you are."

"She is an inspiration to me," I said, though I have no idea why. "How did you meet?"

"My sister Marge plays mahjong with your aunt every week," Alan said. "She invited me on one of their bus trips to Atlantic City. By the time your aunt rolled her first hard eight, I was smitten."

"She is a piece of work."

"She's a joy," he said. "She keeps me young."

Then a commotion arose behind me. It was Ada and four other old women, making so much noise it sounded like a kennel.

"Here he is," my aunt was saying, "this is my nephew."

"You're the one from the radio?" one of the ladies said.

"That's me."

"That show is terrible," she said, stone-faced. "It is nothing but drivel."

"A lot of people feel that way," I said.

"I'm sure."

Then they were on their way out again, just as quickly as they'd come.

"I'll send Harry in and we'll get started," my aunt shouted.

Alan and I were alone again. "Who is Harry?" I asked him.

"My son."

"Let me ask you something. The woman who said my show was drivel, was that Fern Cohen?"

"No," he said. "That was my sister."

I sat on the edge of the bed next to him. "Let me ask you something else," I said, leaning a bit closer. "Why are you two getting married?"

"I thought we'd better before she starts showing."

Then he laughed amiably before I became too confused. "I'm just fooling with you, of course."

"Why?"

"Why does *anyone* get married?"

"I mean at your age," I said.

"This is the youngest we're ever going to be."

I was just thinking that I really liked Alan Glickstein, and that he might be the most normal member of my family, when he spoke again.

"Can you do me a favor?" he asked.

"Of course."

He pulled a plastic bag from the breast pocket of his jacket.

"With my arthritis I have trouble opening these and they're my favorite," he said. "Would you mind cracking a few for me?"

They were pistachio nuts.

"I'd be happy to," I said, and cracked open a few shells. I had a few myself, too. They were salty and left a green stain on my fingers. "Alan," I said, "I'm very glad to be here for this."

Then the bedroom door opened and a guy about my age burst in, screaming.

"YOU'RE NOT SUPPOSED TO EAT NUTS!"

He jammed his hand in the old man's mouth and rooted around, the way my wife did when my son almost swallowed a marble. Then he turned to me and screamed directly into my face. "HE'S NOT SUPPOSED TO EAT NUTS! ARE YOU TRYING TO KILL HIM?"

I turned to Alan. "I can't believe you just threw me under the bus like that," I said.

He replied with a terrific shrug that said, *When it comes to pistachios, it's every man for himself.*

I extended my hand to the younger man. "My name is Michael, I'm Ada's nephew. I'm very sorry if I did something wrong here."

"I'm Alan's son," he said. "What did he offer you? Did he offer you money?"

"He didn't offer me anything," I said. "He just asked politely."

"If I want to eat nuts," Alan said, "I'll eat nuts."

"YOU ARE NOT SUPPOSED TO EAT NUTS!"

I left without another word and went to the hall to find my aunt. She was smiling the same way she did that time she hit the daily double at Yonkers.

"He tricked you?" she asked.

"I guess so."

"He's a smart one."

"Why can't he eat nuts?" I asked.

"Michael, at his age you can't eat anything," she said. "That's why you should eat as much as you can now."

"I will."

"Stay after the wedding," she said. "We'll start with the brisket."

"He isn't going to die from those nuts, is he?" I asked.

"We're all going to die from something," she said. "For him, the over/under is ten years."

"I'll take the over," I said.

Then I watched my aunt marry Alan Glickstein. And when everyone else had gone, we sat down and ate the brisket. It was so soft we could have used spoons. I always tell myself these moments are going to change me but they almost never do, so I won't pretend everything is going to be different when I wake up tomorrow morning. But I do know one thing: I'm definitely going to pick up some pistachios this week. They were really good.

*   *   *

I went to see Dr. Gray this morning and I don't know if I'm going back.

I mean, ever.

Here's what happened: It started with this journal. The last time I went to see her she asked if she could read parts of what I have written. She said she thought she would get a clearer picture of my feelings if she read about them. She went so far as to imply that I am not truthful in our sessions, which I do not resent as much as I simply disagree with. I have always been honest with Dr. Gray. Perhaps not terribly forthcoming, but always honest.

Anyway, I sent her the journal and then today when I got to her office she had the most bizarre expression on her face, like when my son bit into a grape tomato expecting a regular grape.

"Michael," she said, "I have read these pages and, quite frankly, I'm shocked."

I don't know if you have any experience in this, but that is about the *last* thing you want to hear from someone who's just read your diary.

"What do you mean?"

"It's all made up," she said. "There is hardly a shred of you in here."

"Well, Doc, you know what I always say: Never let the facts get in the way of a good story."

"When do you say that?" she asked.

"On the radio."

"Michael, in case you haven't figured this out, you're *not* on the radio when you're here. I'm *not* part of your audience. This is an inappropriate place to be testing material."

"I'm sorry."

"This is a place for honesty and introspection," she said. "If you cannot be honest with yourself, how can you expect to feel better?"

Maybe that's just it. Maybe I don't expect to feel better.

"Doc," I said, "it isn't made up. It's all true. At least, in the way that anything is true when you host a talk show. I just exaggerated the interesting parts and eliminated the chatter. But the sum total of it, in my opinion, is pretty close to accurate."

She looked at me sternly. (And she gives a pretty good stern look.) "Why do you continue coming to see me?"

"What?"

"It's obvious you don't believe this is helping you," she said. "It's obvious you don't believe it *can* help you. We are both busy people; don't you think we have better things to do with our time than have you test out material in this office?"

I tried to respond to that but my voice caught in my throat. What

I wanted to say was "Everything is so much easier on the radio." But I didn't. In fact, I didn't say anything at all.

"I want you to think about why you come here," she said. "And then I want you to think about whether you shouldn't just stop."

I shuffled out dejectedly. And now I'm doing what she asked. I'm thinking about it. Why *do* I go see her? Could it be just because she listens to me? Could it be that I just need *someone* to listen to me when I'm not on the radio?

No, there must be other reasons.

I also think I continue to see her because I know it isn't her that is failing. It's me. She's doing her job; I'm just not getting it. She always says it's about sports and the children. She's probably right.

But *what* is it?

What is it about sports and the children that keeps me in a constant state of unrest?

Maybe it's that sometimes I feel so profoundly disappointed by the world of sports that it makes me question who I am. All my life, sports have grounded me. In times of confusion or of sorrow, through whatever turbulence I have encountered, sports have always been able to bring me down safely. (A woman dumped me over the telephone one time, sort of broke my heart. The first thing I did was pick up my copy of *Sports Illustrated* off the nightstand. Somehow, I knew that reading about Joe Montana was all the assurance I needed that everything would be all right.)

I've been able to depend on that comfort all my life; I don't know what I would do without it. But lately I feel I am losing it. I feel these games I love are slipping so far away I can barely find them through the smoke and haze of labor stoppages and drug arrests and doping scandals.

And if sports have become less important, then what have *I* become?

That makes me feel small. It makes me feel like my kids aren't going to understand sports as I have. And if they can't, maybe they won't be able to understand *me*. I feel I need to save sports, however much I can, for my children. So they can understand how wonderful it can be. So they can understand their dad.

Could the whole bloody thing be as simple as that?

I'm not sure. But I'm not going to give up trying to find out. And I'm going to leave Dr. Gray a message right now, to tell her I plan to be there at the usual time next week.

●　　●　　●

I had two epiphanies this weekend.

The first came on Saturday, and I feel conflicted having gained so much enlightenment from such a tragedy. You see, my wife's cousin Sheila died. Remember her? The one with the green shoes. And the *other* wedding, the one I didn't want to go to because I had tickets to a football game.

She was killed in a car accident.

Horrible.

Saturday was the funeral. It was unimaginable, the worst I've ever been to by far. Probably because the victim was the youngest. I am accustomed to funerals for old people. I am accustomed to being greeted with a knowing nod, a gentle handshake, handkerchiefs clutched tightly but not overly used. I am accustomed to eulogies that celebrate lives lived well, or at least lived long. I am accustomed to offering praise along with condolences, passing along a lesson learned, sharing a wistful laugh over a cherished memory.

There were none of those at this funeral.

These were faces washed over in disbelief, scrubbed clean of emotion and understanding. This was about the sort of anguish for which there is no solace, no explanation. This was about anger more than sadness, pain more than tears. It was the first funeral I have ever been to that was more about questions than it was about answers.

When the service ended my wife tugged at my arm, nudging me gently toward the family, imploring me with her eyes. We were in the receiving line, closer to the front than the back. Soon we would be face-to-face with the dead woman's parents. My wife nodded slowly. *Think*, she was saying. *Think of something to say.*

As we waited our turn, all I could think about was the rabbi's eulogy. He'd said that the quality of one's life is judged not by how long it was lived but how well. And he offered no explanation for everyone's disbelief. He just said there are times when we have questions we cannot answer, and the ultimate test of our faith is to believe that there *is* an answer, even though we could never fathom what it might be.

When it was our turn I extended my hand toward Sheila's father but he pushed it away and pulled me close, hugging me hard. He's a man I do not know well, but I'll never forget the day we spent together at a football game, the day of his daughter's wedding. I wanted to tell him how fondly I remember that day, how often I still think of it, even after all this time. I wanted him to know how much he helped me that day, how much I learned. I wanted to tell him how much that insignificant football game has meant to me.

But he just kept hugging me for what seemed a very long time. I don't have any idea how long it really was. Any sense of perspective was washed away in the sound of his breathing, and the scratchy feel of his wool suit, and the intermingling smells of aftershave and cigarettes. He is a giant of a man, much bigger than I am, and his embrace enveloped me completely; I'm sure from the outside I was barely visible. Then he let go and I stepped back and opened my mouth, but nothing came out. I just stood, shaking my head, searching for a voice, staring at his tie, at his collar, at the tiny patch of hair beneath his jaw he had missed when he'd shaved.

"Next year, my Eagles are going all the way."

At first, I wasn't sure who said that. The voice was strange, distant. It was him, of course, and now I looked into his eyes and immediately wished I hadn't. They looked unlike any eyes I've ever seen on a man. They looked like a shark's eyes, like they might roll over and go black at any moment. They were pleading with me to tell him this wasn't real, that someday he would awaken from this nightmare. He wanted me to tell him this was not what his life was going to be from now on. He looked as though I was the only one in the room who *could* tell him that. And maybe I was.

"I'm not crazy about your defense."

My voice sounded deep and strong in my own ears, the way it does on the radio.

"If my quarterback keeps getting better, we won't need that much defense."

His eyebrows rose as he spoke, one at a time. His face was still drawn and pale, but there was life in his expression.

"You could use another playmaker on offense," I said.

"You could say that about a lot of teams."

"I know, but without a big-time defense you're more vulnerable than most."

There was a line behind me, more people than I could see, more than I could imagine, all waiting to pay their respects. But they would have to wait. There would be time for all of that. The rest of his life would be all of that. Right now, we were two guys talking about sports.

"How about the Sixers?" he asked, hopefully.

"I think it's going to be a long year," I said.

It was ten minutes before he put his arms out and hugged me again, even harder this time. I knew what that meant. It meant he was as close to all right as he was going to be today. It meant I had given him the strength to face all those behind me, and all those behind them. It meant: "Thanks for a moment of normalcy, on the worst day of my life."

"I'll be rooting for you," I said.

Then I stepped to the side and watched him receive the next couple. His expression turned cold again the instant they approached. The woman leaned close and whispered something in his ear, and I saw the father's jaw clench and tighten. But his eyes weren't black anymore. They were still red from lack of sleep, and swollen from crying, and the pupils were dilated from whatever tranquilizer was rushing through his veins, keeping him from hurting himself, but they weren't black anymore. So I went over to hug his wife. I knew I could not comfort her the same way I had comforted him, but that was all right. A hug is a hug sometimes.

That was the first epiphany.

The second came this morning, the Sunday morning after the Saturday funeral. It came at the end of an awfully long morning, one of those Sunday mornings only parents of young children can have.

One of those Sunday mornings when your daughter walks into your bedroom much too early because the shadows in her closet spooked her, and then ten minutes later she is happily asleep beside your wife and you are hopelessly awake. One of those Sunday mornings when you take the kids to the diner for breakfast because you are a masochist, and your son pours orange juice over his head and your daughter cries because we don't eat chicken fingers for breakfast, and they are both clanging the silverware on the tabletop, which is torturous at the best of times but particularly sucks now because you drank too much after the funeral and the pain behind your eyes is spreading like molten lava.

One of those Sundays when after the diner you take the kids to the playground and chase them across the monkey bars and through the sandbox and up the rock-climbing wall and down the slide, and one of them is crying because he scraped his knee and the other is pouting because Alexa is allowed to chew gum. One of those Sundays when you ask the kids what they want for lunch and she says Chicken Mc-Nuggets and he says pizza, and you know you can't do either because your wife will give you the business if they eat that crap. One of those Sundays with a birthday party to take your daughter to, which means twenty minutes of debate over what she will wear. ("*You cannot wear pink tights with a green dress. You cannot wear tights at all. It is freezing outside. You must wear pants.*")

It was one of those Sundays only parents have. And all I wanted to do was watch golf on TV. The only thought that kept me going through the diner and the playground and the party was that soon I would be home watching the end of the golf.

So, finally, after everyone whined their way through turkey and cheese and spent a half hour making a mess of the family room, both little ones went upstairs for a nap. And then my wife turned my blood ice-cold.

"You know, Lourdes is off this week," she said to me. "So we need to go to the supermarket."

Not the supermarket. Not today, of all days.

Then the miracle happened.

"You look tired," she said. "I'll go."

I couldn't believe it. (I still can't.) I watched in stunned silence as she gathered herself and grabbed the car keys and then she was gone. And it was quiet in my house. I could hear my own footsteps on the wood floors. I could hear a distant car horn. I could hear everything and I couldn't hear anything, both at the same time.

I basked in the silence for a moment and then kicked off my shoes and jumped on the couch. And the first words I heard from the television made my heart sink.

"If Ernie Els makes this putt, he wins the championship."

Oh no!

I had missed the entire thing. Els was lining up a putt that couldn't have been more than six feet. He makes those with his eyes closed. This was going to be all over right now.

Then another miracle happened.

"Els leaves it short! He'll tap that in for par and we're headed to a three-hole play-off!"

A play-off! Ernie Els and someone else (I didn't even care who) were going to play three more holes of golf—just for me. Three more holes while my kids napped and my wife was at the supermarket. Three more holes while I ignored the phone and the doorbell and my BlackBerry and my neighbor's lawn mower. Three more holes while I sat with my feet on the ottoman and a cold bottle of ginger ale in my hands. There was nothing on earth I would rather do than watch those three holes. Nowhere I would rather be. I wanted it to go on forever.

When I was a little kid, someone asked me what I wanted to be when I grew up. I think I said that if I could just be around sports all the time, it would always be fun. It would never seem like work. And as I sit on this couch right now, I realize that little kid was right. It *is* fun to be around sports. It doesn't have to feel like work. At just the right times, there is nothing better in the whole wide world. I guess Tom Sawyer had it right all along.

EPILOGUE
After the Supermarket

May 2005

THIS MORNING I awoke to find a gorgeous, sunny day—the first of the season. To me, this is the best day of the year: when you awaken and find that summer has arrived. This day smells and tastes fresher than any other, and there's only one place it should ever be spent.

The beach.

"Oh, what a beautiful morning," I said to my wife, who was only barely awake. "Oh, what a beautiful day!"

"If you say you've got a beautiful feeling," she said wearily, "you're sleeping in the guest room tonight."

"Let's take the kids to the beach," I said.

"I have to go shopping today," she said. "The kids have no clothes for summer."

Every time the kids need clothes she somehow ends up with new Jimmy Choos, but today I didn't care. Let her shop. I was taking the kids to the beach.

"Just be sure you bring hats," she said. "Don't forget the hats."

My wife has read one too many articles about skin cancer. Actually, she has read one too many articles about everything, which is why I never leave the house without sunblock, mosquito repellent, waterless soap, tick repellent, nonperishable food products, a two-day supply of water, and—above all else—hats.

"I won't," I said, and went to wake the children.

"Don't forget the hats."

It took nearly an hour to get them both dressed and fed and into the car, and then we were off to the beach. It was not until I had parked and unloaded the umbrella and blankets and shovels and pails and water wings and bathing suits and goggles and masks and snorkels and fins that it hit me.

I had forgotten the hats.

Suddenly, a beautiful day took on a foreboding air. The brilliant sunshine ceased to feel welcome on my skin. Now I felt it eating away my flesh. But I did not panic. There is a little shop at the beach. Certainly, they would sell baseball caps.

And I'm sure they do, when they're open. But this weekend they were not. Summer came well before Memorial Day this year, so all the shops were deserted, as was the snack bar. There was no sign of life anywhere.

Still, I didn't panic. All I needed to do was coat their little heads in sunscreen—I mean *slather* it on. That would protect them, even without hats. Who would ever know?

Then I heard my daughter's voice.

"Stephanie!"

Leave it to my five-year-old to know someone at the beach. Sure enough, there was little Stephanie walking toward us, hand in hand with her brother, Ethan, and their gossipy mom, Carol. They live on our street and Carol is the neighborhood's Gladys Kravitz. There is no one whose business she does not mind. If I did not act immediately, she would no doubt call my wife from the car on her way home.

"Hi, Carol, how are you?"

"Good. I just saw Michael and the kids at the beach."

"Were they wearing hats?"

"No, that's what I called to tell you."

As luck would have it, they had set up their beach towels just a few yards from ours, and all the kids ran off together to play.

"So, how's everything in the sports world these days?" Carol asked.

"I'm going to the car to get hats," I said.

There was a real chance there would be two hats just lying around in the car. (Frankly, there was a chance Jimmy Hoffa was lying around in the car. There isn't anything you might not find if you dug through the car my kids are in every day.) I could see the disappointment on nosy Carol's face. I'm sure she thought she had caught me without hats. Not only would she have told my wife, it would have been all over town by nightfall. The woman moves information faster than the Internet.

Back at the car I came to a fork in the road. A real dilemma. A crossroads, of sorts. Because sure enough there *were* two hats.

Both pink.

With pictures of Barbie on them.

I remember where we got them: at a Barbie-themed birthday party, where they were distributed as party favors. We were among the last to leave and the mother of the birthday girl told me to take an extra. "You never know when you may need it," she said.

So my options were clear: Either I could pack the kids up and head for home, or I could put my two-year-old son into a pink Barbie baseball cap.

What would you have done? I ask now because I have time, a luxury I didn't enjoy at the beach. With every second that passed, my children's vulnerable scalps were being exposed to harmful ultraviolet rays. Not to mention the stopwatch nosy Carol was probably running; anything over three minutes, I have no doubt she would have been on the phone with my wife before I got back to the blankets.

"Hi, Carol, how are you?"

"Good. I just thought you'd want to know the kids have been on the beach without hats for four minutes."

So I acted. I marched back from the car and put that pink Barbie cap right on my little boy's head. And instantly I felt great. The sun felt wonderful again, the rays gently caressing my skin. It was, after all, the first day of summer, the first of what would be so many like this. The air smelled delicious. I could taste the salt in the breeze. Finally, I had encountered the perfect day.

"Hey, aren't you Greeny?"

Oh no.

The voice came from behind me and it was raspy. It was the voice of a sports fan who had drunk one too many beers and smoked one too many cigarettes and probably a few cigars. I turned to find the fellow just about as I expected—tall and thick, probably athletic at one time, but years of beer and buffalo wings had done away with that. He was wearing a Brett Favre jersey with the sleeves cut off, showing a multitude of tattoos, one of which seemed to be a boy shooting a horse.

"Hey, I'm pleased to meecha," he said, wiping his hands on his shorts and extending one for me to shake. "I'm a big fan of the show."

"Thanks," I said, "that's nice of you to say."

"Is this the family you always talk so much about?" he asked. "Are these your kids?"

I took a deep breath and sighed. "Yup," I said. "That's my little girl, she's five, and my son is almost three."

I saw the look of confusion on his face. "That's a boy?"

"His mother told me to make sure he had a hat but I forgot, so he's wearing his sister's hat." The guy didn't look convinced. "You know, to block out the sun from his eyes and stuff."

The fellow nodded. "Let me help you out."

With that, he disappeared so quickly I couldn't tell where he went. I glanced over at Carol.

"Your fans are so classy, Michael," she said.

Then he was back. In one hand was an unopened can of Budweiser. In the other was a baseball cap with my name on it. "I ordered it from your website," he said, dropping it on the blanket beside my son. "He looks like he needs it more than I do."

Then he was gone again, before I could even thank him. I picked up the hat and examined it. It appeared to be clean, as though it had never been worn before. I put it on my son's head and took the pink Barbie hat and placed it on my own. And I left it there for the entire afternoon, which I must say passed quite happily. The kids dug in the sand and romped in the surf and everyone was tired and smiling when we were done.

When we got home, my wife was at the door with my son's hat in her hands. I recognized the look on her face, that gleeful anger that means she's happy I screwed up because now she can hold it over me for six years. I wish you could have seen her face when her son hopped out of the car with a hat on.

"Mama!"

He raced toward her with his little arms open wide as he could. She picked him up and hugged him, then discreetly tossed the other cap back into the house. I barely caught it out of the corner of my eye.

I carried our little girl over and whispered in her ear. "Give Mommy a big kiss."

It wasn't until later, with the kids bathed and fed and tucked into bed, that my wife asked about our day at the beach.

"It was terrific," I said, and left it at that. "How was the shopping?"

"They didn't have much for the kids."

"No?"

"I got myself a few things."

I smiled. We were out on the porch, basking in the glory of the first evening of summer. I was drinking a brandy and puffing on a Dunhill and the sun was just setting, casting an orange haze that matched perfectly the glowing tip of my cigar. I looked over and found that she too had relaxed. She was sipping white wine and leaning back in her chair, eyes closed. The smoke from my cigar was winding about her, drifting off into the stillness of a warm night. She looked beautiful, prettier even than when I'd married her. I could tell she had forgotten all about the hats, and the fight we didn't have over them. And so had I. And there isn't any question it was my favorite day of the year.

Acknowledgments

BEFORE I BEGIN trying to express my gratitude to all those who deserve it, I want to first make one hundred percent clear that all the events described in the preceding pages actually took place in my life, with the exception of those few that did not.

That said, I would first like to thank my agent, Jacques de Spoelberch, for his guidance, his friendship, and the three strokes a side he is going to give me from now on.

I would also like to thank Gene Young, who brought me to Jacques, and who taught me to write, as much as anyone did.

My thanks to all at Random House and Villard. In particular, Adam Korn, who was an enthusiastic supporter from the start. And I hardly know what to say to Mark Tavani. It would take a far more eloquent writer to properly express my gratitude. Suffice it to say, this would never have happened without you, Mark. Thanks.

Thanks, too, to all my friends and colleagues at ESPN. Especially Mike Golic, to whom I owe more than I could ever repay. Mike, you're the most dedicated father I have ever known. Of the countless things I have learned from you, that's the most important. Thanks, big guy. And to Justin Craig, Liam Chapman, Curtis "Joaquin" Kaplan, and Bob Picozzi, the cast and crew of *Mike and Mike in the Morning:* Every day I spend in your company is a privilege.

I would also like to thank the many friends who may have recognized themselves in these pages, like Jackie Harris-Hochberg and Robert Hochberg, Jane Green and David Burke, Kim and Mark Shapiro, Leslie and Harvey Riback, Kate Neisser and Stephen Burns, Rona Stein and Ed Kerman, David Lloyd, Angelo Devita, Dezrine Brady, Dr. Victoria J. Boies, Claudia Slocum, Rick Schuham, Lou Oppenheim, and George Dusak, the bravest sports fan I know.

But more than anything, this book is about family, and I am grateful to be blessed with so many families that make up my own. All my love and thanks to Eric, Scott, Shawn, and Lewis Ingall, Bea Gray Steponate and Frank Steponate, Lillian Pinchoff and Harry Hershey. And to my brother and closest friend, Douglas Greenberg, and his wife, Jill Brenegan, as they begin this journey themselves. And, especially, to my parents, Harriet and Arnold Greenberg, for teaching me to appreciate writing, and for a lifetime of unconditional support.

About the Author

MIKE GREENBERG is co-host of *Mike and Mike in the Morning* on ESPN Radio and an anchor on ESPN's *SportsCenter.* He is a graduate of the Medill School of Journalism at Northwestern University. Greenberg lives outside New York City with his wife and two children. This is his first book.